MW01199874

HIKE
THE GOLDEN GATE
NATIONAL PARKLANDS

Hike. Contemplate what makes you happy and what makes you happier still. Follow a trail or blaze a new one. **Hike.** Think about what you can do to expand your life and someone else's. **Hike.** Slow down. Gear up. **Hike.** Connect with friends. Re-connect with nature.

Hike. Shed stress. Feel blessed. **Hike** to remember. **Hike** to forget. **Hike** for recovery. **Hike** for discovery. **Hike.** Enjoy the beauty of providence. **Hike.** Share the way, The Hiker's Way, on the long and winding trail we call life.

HIKE
THE GOLDEN GATE
NATIONAL PARKLANDS

BY
JOHN McKINNEY

TheTrailmaster.com

HIKE the Golden Gate National Parklands: Best Day Hikes by John McKinney

HIKE the Golden Gate National Parklands ©2022 The Trailmaster, Inc.

Book Design by Lisa DeSpain
Cartography by Mark Chumley
HIKE Series Editor: Cheri Rae

Published by Olympus Press and The Trailmaster, Inc.
TheTrailmaster.com (Visit our site for a complete listing of all Trailmaster publications, products, and services.)

Although The Trailmaster, Inc. and the author have made every attempt to ensure that information in this book is accurate, they are not responsible for any loss, damage, injury, or inconvenience that may occur to you while using this information. You are responsible for your own safety; the fact that an activity or trail is described in this book does not mean it will be safe for you. Trail conditions can change from day to day; always check local conditions and know your limitations.

CONTENTS

I San Francisco

The Glorious Golden Gate:
View it from many vantage points
on national parkland trails.

EVERY TRAIL TELLS A STORY.

INTRODUCTION

Hike Ocean Beach, Baker Beach and Muir Beach, Fort Mason, Fort Funston and Fort Point, Gerbode Valley, Oakwood Valley, Tennessee Valley, Muir Woods, the Presidio, Golden Gate Promenade, Alcatraz Island...ah, the wonderful Golden Gate National Parklands!

The Golden Gate National Recreation Area (GGNRA) protects 82,027 acres of what the National Park Service calls "ecologically and historically significant landscape surrounding the San Francisco Bay Area." With more than 12 million visitors per year, GGNRA is the most visited national parkland in the U.S. About a million more visitors flock to Muir Woods National Monument.

Many visitors have a grand time without realizing they did so on national parkland. A lunch at Cliff House, a walk along Lovers' Lane through the Presidio, a theater performance at Fort Mason—these are just a few of the many pleasures available within the boundaries of the park.

The old slogan "Parks are for people" definitely applies to GGNRA. There's no statistical breakdown for the percentage of visitors who are hikers, but it would be a safe to say GGNRA is among the most popular places to hike in the U.S

One of the largest urban parks in the world, GGNRA is more than two-and-a-half times the size of the city of San Francisco. The park is not one continuous area, but a diverse collection of natural, historical and recreational areas that extend from southern San Mateo County to northern Marin County, and includes significant portions of San Francisco's shoreline.

My hike leader experience helped me understand why so many hikers leave their hearts in San Francisco. When I led hikes in the area for The Wayfarers, an upscale walking vacation company, response from the hikers (who hailed from across the U.S. and from Europe) in my charge to the GGNRA was enthusiastic to say the least. The hike across the historic Presidio to Lands End, then over the Golden Gate Bridge...the hike across the Marin Headlands...the hike from Tennessee Valley to Muir Beach...well, you get the idea!

All that greenery amidst the scenery is impressive. You'll enjoy great photo ops of the Golden Gate Bridge—from the Coastal Trail and Baker Beach, from the Bay shore and the Golden Gate Promenade.

And you must make the once-in-a-lifetime hike over the Golden Gate Bridge. (I thought everybody knew you could walk across the Golden Gate, but that doesn't seem to be the case, even among some well-traveled hikers I've met.)

In addition to the many natural and cultural treasures accessible by trail, what else is special about hiking here?

Easy answer: the fog!

Sometimes the fog "comes in on little cat feet," as Carl Sandburg's poem describes it. Other times,

Creeping in on its cat feet, fog frequently blankets the Bay.

banks of fog roll in rapidly, smothering the city, and vanishing just as quickly.

Fog is an enduring feature of San Francisco summers. The expression, "the coldest winter I ever spent was the summer I spent in San Francisco," while wrongly attributed to Mark Twain, is nonetheless as true as it is clever. Among major U.S. cities, San Francisco has the coldest average daily mean, maximum and minimum temperatures for the summer months.

But there's a definite upside to all that Pacific air, which keeps temperatures in a narrow, usually moderate range, with the temperatures rarely rising above 75 degrees F or dipping below 45 degrees F. With temperatures rarely too hot or too cold, GGNRA is blessed with terrific hiking weather all year long!

One of the perks of hiking a national parkland located in and near a metropolis is the easy availability of food and refreshment. Stick with trail mix and water if you must, but know you could start your day with a yummy breakfast burrito and end it with a cool one at a microbrewery. A wide variety of restaurants and delis are located close to trailheads.

While GGNRA's shore is every bit a part of the city of San Francisco, it also offers a feeling of remoteness as well. Preserving the waterfront as public domain during the Real Estate Go-Go years of the 1970s and 1980s, provided San Francisco with a terrific greenbelt sprinkled with historical and cultural attractions.

When the park was created, recreation and the area's natural treasures were top of mind. However, GGNRA has much to offer in the way of historical resources. History-minded hikers can explore a chain of forts, gun batteries and other military sites dating from the Gold Rush to the 1960s. The Presidio, transferred to the National Park Service from the U.S. Army in 1994, has been converted from an Army base to a unique area combining educational and cultural facilities with nature trails and beaches. America's most infamous prison site, Alcatraz Island, is also part of GGNRA. Hikers with an eye for architecture will admire steep-pitched Victorians in the Presidio, and out in Olema Valley. The elaborate brick masonry of Civil War-era Fort Point, the Sutro Bath ruins, and many more buildings offer an insight into San Francico's rich history. The famed Golden Gate Bridge, namesake and centerpiece for the National Recreation Area, can be admired from below at Fort Point, from the ridgetops of the Marin Headlands, and from many more vista points in the GGNRA.

Hiking GGNRA offers an urban-rural-wilderness collage; natural history and social history is often part of the same walk. From the forested ridges, take in San Francisco's skyline; from the city, look toward the bold Marin Headlands. This national parkland

"Tony Bennett's signature song comes to me on the trail: 'I left my heart in San Francisco, high on a hill'."—John McKinney, author.

offers nature nearby. With a short drive or bus ride from San Francisco, you can reach trailheads for hikes that lead across dramatic coastal bluffs, through fern-filled ravines and amidst ancient redwood forests. Hike smart, reconnect with nature and enjoy your hikes in the Golden Gate National Parklands.

Hike on.

—John McKinney

Geography

Geologists tell us San Francisco and the Golden Gate headlands are located on the boundary between two of the earth's mightiest tectonic plates, the North American and Pacific plates. GGNRA's rocky cliffs not only form a background and foreground for photos of the Golden Gate Bridge, but also provide a geologic record of continent-building and the tension between the two plates going back 200 million years.

On a more lyrical note, the geography—this dramatic meeting of land and sea—inspires artists, photographers, musicians, and visitors from all walks of life. In his essay, "Golden Gate: A Hidden Geography," Richard Walker refers to "the geographic magic done by the hand of nature and humankind."

The city and portions of the GGNRA are located on a narrow arm of land next to San Francisco Bay, the largest land-locked harbor in the world. San Francisco is surrounded on three sides by water: the Pacific Ocean, the Golden Gate Strait, and San Francisco Bay. Pacific waters temper San Francisco's weather, keeping temperatures and overall climate unusually consistent and mild year-round. GGNRA's hills, however, create distinct microclimates around them and cause wide variations in temperature and sky conditions in different parts of the park. The famous fog blankets different elevations in varying ways, resulting in complex patterns of mist and sunshine. Most common on summer mornings, the fog rolls in from the cooler ocean and backs up against the hills. In winter, the fog comes from colder inland areas.

Natural History

Let's be honest and admit the term "urban national park" does not suggest an abundance of wildlife and natural treasures. Perhaps surprisingly, though, GGNRA boasts a diversity of ecosystems and thriving populations.

Take a walk along the windy shoreline to Lands End.

GGNRA's varied shoreline includes sand dunes, sandy shores, wetlands and marshes, as well as a rich and rocky intertidal zone. The park features oak woodlands and a redwood forest complete with a lush understory of trillium, redwood sorrel, and sword ferns. Spring wildflowers splash color across prairies and grasslands. Hardy coastal shrubs and chaparral thrive on south-facing slopes despite rocky soils and harsh winds.

More than half of the bird species of North America have been sighted in GGNRA. This abundance of birds is related to the diversity of habitats in the parklands around San Francisco: coastal scrub, grass prairies, sandy and rocky shorelines, creeks and salt marshes, oak woodlands, redwood forests and more.

Marine mammals are often spotted along GGNRA's 60 miles of shore. Watch for whales, seals and sea lions. Keep an eye out for numerous haul-out and pupping locales along the coast.

The park is home to more than 3,000 plant and animal species. Golden Gate National Recreation area and adjacent parklands were designated as the Golden Gate Biosphere Reserve by UNESCO in 1988.

Conservation History

The land now comprising GGNRA had long been under government ownership. American military occupation dating from the 1840s restricted development. As the Army's properties became obsolete for modern defense, they were transferred to the National Park Service.

Park advocates managed to circumvent the requirement that national parklands be contiguous and convinced lawmakers to create Golden Gate National Recreation Area in 1972. During the next three decades, the National Park Service acquired Alcatraz Island, Fort Mason, Fort Funston, Cliff House, Crissy Field, the Presidio and much more.

The Nature Conservancy purchased land in the Marin Headlands from a would-be developer and

A trio of treasures in GGNRA: fabled Cliff House, Seal Rock, and the ruins of the Sutro Baths.

transferred it to GGNRA. Rancho Corral de Tierra, a former Mexican land grant on the San Mateo Peninsula was preserved through the efforts of the Peninsula Open Space Trust.

GGNRA has benefited enormously from the efforts of a stellar nonprofit support organization, the Golden Gate National Parks Conservancy. The hiking experience has been greatly enhanced by the terrific visitor centers at Muir Woods, Marin Headlands and Lands End. The Conservancy has helped improve Crissy Field and sites along the Golden Gate Promenade, and has also improved and signed many park trails.

Administration

Golden Gate National Recreation Area, Building 201, Fort Mason, San Francisco, CA 94123. Call 415-561-4700, visit nps.gov/goga. The Presidio Visitor Center is located at 210 Lincoln Boulevard on the Presidio's Main Post. Call 415-561-4323, visit presidio.gov The robust nonprofit support organization for GGNRA is the Golden Gate National Parks Conservancy. Learn more at parksconservancy.org

Muir Woods National Monument, 1 Muir Woods Rd, Mill Valley, FA 94941, call 415-561-2850, visit nps.gov/muwo.

Transit to Trails

San Francisco's far-reaching transit system enables you to reach the start of nearly every hike in this guide by bus. Getting there can be half the fun for residents and visitors alike.

Even if you can reach the start of a hike by car, you may choose not to drive to the trailhead. Many of the parklands highlighted in this guide experience significant congestion and scarce parking during peak use periods, so public transit can be a great option for hikers. Basic public transit information is available at 511.org.

The Golden Gate National Parks Conservancy (parksconservancy.org) features a planning tool and interactive map and links up with Transit and Trails

Most GGNRA trailheads are easily accessible by transit.

(transitandtrails.org), which helps connect you to parks and open spaces, find and plan hikes. The site also provided public transportation info, plus directions to walk, bike, or drive to the start of a hike.

The PresidiGo Shuttle system (presidiobus. com) is a great (and free!) service for hikers bound for trails in and near the Presidio. "Downtown" and "Around the Park" PresidiGo Shuttle routes are integrated with Google Maps trip planning system.

The Downtown route makes stops at the Presidio Transit Center on Main Post, the Letterman District, Union Street/ Van Ness Avenue, Embarcadero BART, and the Transbay Terminal.

Around the Park shuttle has a very popular Crissy Field Route serving the northern Presidio including the Main Post, Golden Gate Bridge, Fort Scott and Letterman District. The Presidio Hills Route serves the Letterman District, Main Post, Inspiration Point, Washington Boulevard, Baker Beach, and more. Both routes originate at the Presidio Transit Center and connect with MUNI and Golden Gate Transit at several locations.

Wildflower-framed views of the Golden Gate Bridge, a highlight of hiking the national parklands near San Francisco.

EVERY TRAIL TELLS A STORY.

I

SAN FRANCISCO

HIKE ON.

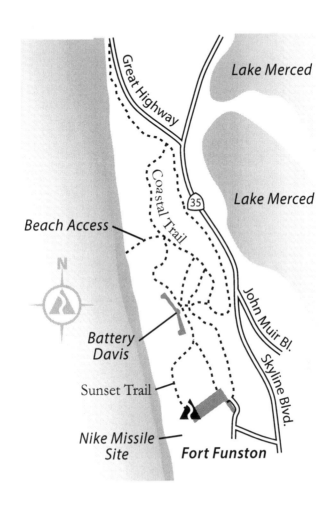

Lake Merced

Great Highway

Lake Merced

35

Coastal Trail

Beach Access

John Muir Bl.

Skyline Blvd.

N

Battery
Davis

Sunset Trail

Nike Missile
Site

Fort Funston

FORT FUNSTON

SUNSET TRAIL

To Battery Davis is 0.8 mile round trip; to Beach Access is 1.4 miles round trip; to Ocean Beach is 1.8 miles round trip

Bold, windswept headlands and soaring sand dunes characterize Fort Funston, an unusual stretch of shoreline that extends south from Ocean Beach. Sunset Trail, the California coast's first wheelchair-accessible pathway, explores this unique pocket of the Golden Gate National Recreation Area.

Several paths meander over the bluffs and connect to the dunes and Funston Beach. Coastal Trail leads to Ocean Beach. Funston's pathways are wildly popular with dogs and their owners.

When Funston was founded in the early 1900s, it resembled a West Coast-style frontier fort. Over the years, ever-more powerful armaments were added—most notably Battery Davis, a heavily reinforced gun emplacement built in 1938. The barrels alone of the battery's 16-inch guns tipped the scale at 146 tons apiece.

Military experts, pleased with the construction, established Battery Davis as the model for all 16-inch gun emplacements built around the U.S.

During World War II, Fort Funston became a base for even heavier weaponry. A Nike missile site was constructed atop the bluffs.

Fort Funston is a more peaceful place these days. Former barracks house the Fort Funston environmental education center, and now host armies of schoolchildren. Disturbed dunes have been re-vegetated with native plants.

The skies above the old fort are filled with friendly aircraft. Tall bluffs combined with dependable Pacific breezes make Fort Funston one of North America's more renowned hang-gliding spots. A wooden observation deck perched on a hillside by the parking lot offers good views of the hang-gliders as well as GGNRA's enticing shoreline.

Sunset Trail visits Battery Davis. Hikers can add to this short walk by joining other Funston paths or by making a longer loop back to the trailhead via the beach. The beach route is best at low tide.

DIRECTIONS: Fort Funston is located about 4.5 miles south of Cliff House at the south end of Ocean Beach. From San Francisco, head south on Great

Highway, continuing as the highway becomes Skyline Boulevard at Lake Merced. About 0.4 mile south of John Muir Drive, turn west off Skyline into the Fort Funston parking lot. If you're headed northbound on Skyline Boulevard, make a U-turn at John Muir Drive and head back south to the park entrance.

THE HIKE: The trail begins near a hang-glider launch and viewing platform and leads past Battery Davis. Descend to a junction with Coastal Trail, head north and soon intersect Funston Beach Trail. This short access trail crosses low, yellow lupine- and beach strawberry-dotted dunes to the beach.

Coastal Trail extends north along the inland side of the dunes (aka "Sensitive Habitat"). Nearing Skyline Boulevard, the trail turns toward shore and heads northbound to Ocean Beach and a parking area along Great Highway.

Putting the fun into Fort Funston: dogs are definitely allowed on the trails!

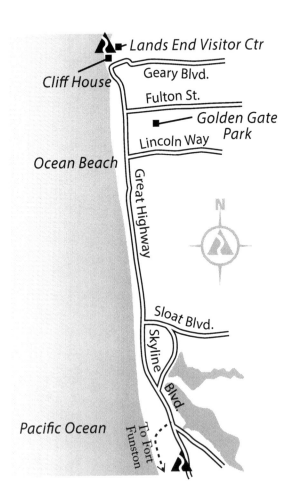

Lands End Visitor Ctr

Cliff House

Geary Blvd.

Fulton St.

Golden Gate Park

Lincoln Way

Ocean Beach

Great Highway

N

Sloat Blvd.

Skyline Blvd.

Pacific Ocean

To Fort Funston

OCEAN BEACH

OCEAN BEACH TRAIL

To Fort Funston is 6 miles round trip

San Francisco is known as the "City by the Bay" not as the "City by the Beach." And yet the city is most definitely bordered by a beach, Ocean Beach, a white sand strand adjacent to Golden Gate Park.

The biggest knock on Ocean Beach is its inhospitable weather—even by San Francisco standards. For that reason, the beach remained largely undeveloped during the city's early building booms and, even in modern times, no high-rises were built along the beach.

Summer fog can mean beach temperatures in the low 50s, which definitely discourages tourists and many natives. Nevertheless there are some great days to take a beach hike in the spring and fall and wonderful "beach days" all year around. Ocean Beach is the place for hanging with friends and family, oceanside picnics and for (strictly regulated) beach fires in designated firepits.

Frigid waters and hazardous currents discourage all but the most experienced surfers. But the Ocean Beach surf community is a passionate one. Look for the locals surfing the roughest and most northern part of the beach known as Kelly's Cove.

Extending between Cliff House and Fort Funston, San Francisco's major sand strand is long (3.5 miles) and wide, and a favorite of joggers, exercise walkers, and surf fishers. Considering its in-town location, Ocean Beach usually offers more solitude than you'd reasonably expect.

Those desiring a longer beach hike than the three-mile jaunt from the parking area on Great Highway south to Fort Funston can easily add longer options. Starting from Cliff House or Lands End Visitor Center adds 0.5 mile or so to the walk. (A multiuse path parallels Great Highway and offers an alternative travel route along Ocean Beach.) The intrepid can continue past Fort Funston to Thornton Beach and even farther south to Mussel Rock on the outskirts of Pacifica.

DIRECTIONS: Ocean Beach parking is located right off Great Highway about one mile south of its intersection with Geary Boulevard. If you're lucky, you'll snag one of the parking spots (free) below Cliff House. Unless it's a rare sunny beach day, parking is usually available.

THE HIKE: From the vista point just below Cliff House, walk down the sidewalk to the beach and continue on the sand. Views out to sea and over the shoulder toward Pt. Reyes are inspiring. Inland, the hiker's attention is attracted by the two 75-foot-high Dutch windmills in Golden Gate Park. On a gray day, perhaps with a storm brewing, Ocean Beach with its seawall could pass for a North Sea scene and make even a native Netherlander nostalgic.

The beach widens and tranquility increases thanks to the dunes that line the strand. In the early days of San Francisco, it was not Great Highway but extensive sand dunes that separated Ocean Beach from the city.

At Ocean Beach's southernmost parking lot, you can join Coastal Trail, which leads back of the dunes and then up the bluffs to Fort Funston.

Ocean Beach usually offers more solitude than you might expect from a sand strand so close to the city.

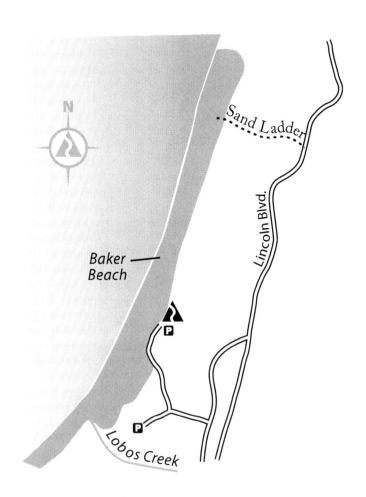

BAKER BEACH

BAKER BEACH TRAIL

2 miles round trip

On this hike to and along Baker Beach, get amazing photo ops of the Bay and Golden Gate Bridge from many different vantage points, including a high view from the Coastal Trail and a straight-on view from the beach. At day's end, the bridge and nearby hills turn shades of gold, orange and red.

Extending a mile below the rugged cliffs on the Presidio's western shoreline, Baker Beach extends southward from Golden Gate Point (where Golden Gate Bridge connects with the peninsula) to the upscale neighborhood of Seacliff. Look for dolphins and harbor seals in the surf, a good environment for marine mammals but not for humans; rip currents and rough waves make Baker Beach unsafe for swimming.

Baker Beach highlights include a picnic area (surrounded by sand dunes sheltered from the wind by a cypress grove). From the north end of the Baker Beach parking lot, walk over to Battery Chamberlin, where a 50-ton, six-inch "disappearing gun" like the kind that defended San Francisco's coast in the early 1900s. Demonstrations of the big gun occur on the first full weekend of each month. Visitors can explore an underground ammunition room which feature exhibits about San Francisco's coastal defenses. (For more info, contact the Presidio Visitor Center.)

The Baker Beach environs are known for its unique dune plants and serpentine rock formations (California's state rock). Far from being a sterile environment, the dunes host a distinct flora that has adapted to challenging conditions. California fore-dune flora includes yellow sand verbena, sagewort and silver beach bur.

Along with the natural scene, there is the *au naturel* scene. Nudists have long been part of the scene; in particular the northern part of Baker Beach attracts clothing-optional sunbathers.

If the coast is fog-bound, only a few fishermen and (warmly and fully dressed) beach hikers frequent the beach. On sunny weekends, though, it's a challenge to find a parking place.

Baker Beach is a destination and departure point for a number of Presidio trails: Lobos Creek Valley Trail, California Coastal Trail, Battery to Bluffs Trail and the "Sand Ladder."

DIRECTIONS: From Highway 101 northbound, take the Presidio/Golden Gate exit. Turn right on Lincoln Boulevard and drive 1.1 mile to the Baker Beach turnoff. Look for curbside parking along Bowley Street and Gibson Street, a modest parking lot off Gibson and a larger lot at the end of Battery Chamberlin Road.

THE HIKE: If you wander down-coast you'll come to Lobos Creek, which flows into the Pacific at the south end Baker Beach.

Keep and eye out for birds—cormorants, pigeon guillemots and brown pelicans offshore and Western gulls, sanderlings and willets foraging on shore.

At its north end, Baker Beach ends at a rocky point. Just on the other side, is another sand strand—Marshall's Beach. To hike there from Baker Beach, ascend the "Sand Ladder" to the California Coastal Trail and a quick connection to Battery to Bluffs Trail.

Great photo ops of the bridge from Baker Beach.

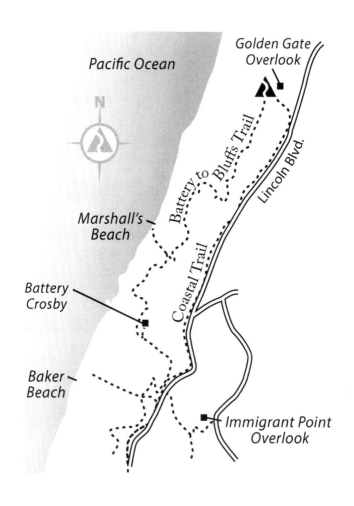

Pacific Ocean

Golden Gate
Overlook

N

Battery to Bluffs Trail

Lincoln Blvd.

Marshall's
Beach

Coastal Trail

Battery
Crosby

Baker
Beach

Immigrant Point
Overlook

TheTrailmaster.com

Stairways to Coastal Heaven

Batteries to Bluffs, Immigrant Point Trails

From Golden Gate Overlook to Immigrant Point via Marshall's Beach is 1.5 miles round trip

For the city walker, San Francisco offers superb stair walks up and down its hills and through its neighborhood. The city has some great "stair hikes," too. Two memorable trails—Batteries to Bluffs and Immigrant Point—on the western edge of the Presidio are coastal versions of the city's famed stair walks.

Batteries to Bluffs Trail leads along the rugged cliffs, serving up fabulous vistas of the Golden Gate Bridge. A spur trail leads to isolated Marshall's Beach. A short jaunt on the Coastal Trail connects to the pathway to Immigrant Point.

You can sure get in a good workout on Immigrant Point/Coastal Connector Trail, as it's officially known. The trail features exactly 217 steps; the total of 1,000 steps includes 783 more steps on the pathway in between the wooden steps.

At Immigrant Point Overlook, enjoy far-reaching views of the Golden Gate Bridge, the Marin Headlands and the wide blue Pacific. Reflect a moment on the coastline that has greeted generations of immigrants.

Golden Gate Overlook, which opened in 2012 as the Golden Gate Bridge celebrated its 75th anniversary, provides a stunning view of the two towers of the Bridge in alignment.

DIRECTIONS: Park at Golden Gate Overlook, located off Lincoln Boulevard, between Langdon Court and Merchant Road. South of the overlook, find parking for about eight cars on the coast side of Lincoln opposite the start of the trail to Immigrant Point.

THE HIKE: Walk south from the overlook past Battery Godfrey and Battery West to the signed junction with Batteries to Bluffs Trail. Descend stairs and trail to a viewpoint and grand views of the ships entering and exiting the Golden Gate. Continue the descent to a little creek, a short and narrow connector trail and a last set of stairs to Marshall's Beach.

Serpentine-cliff bordered Marshall's Beach offers stunning vistas (particularly at sunset) north to the Golden Gate Bridge and the Marin Headlands. Rugged and secluded, this beach seems like an unofficial nude beach.

Now it's upward on the B2B Trail and lots more stairs, with handrails no less. Ascend over the top of Battery Crosby and climb some more to meet Coastal Trail and Lincoln Boulevard.

Carefully cross Lincoln Boulevard to the start of the trail to Immigrant Point Overlook. Near the beginning of the trail is a short bridge and a bench (catch your breath before going up all those stairs). On the ascent amidst pine and eucalyptus trees, enjoy vistas of the Marin Headlands and Point Bonita Lighthouse to the north, and to Seacliff and the Baker Beach bluffs to the south.

Relax on the benches, enjoy the great views from the Immigrant Point, and descend.

For a quicker way back, hike Coastal Trail, which leads along Lincoln Boulevard past Pacific Overlook to Golden Gate Overlook.

View busy international shipping lanes from Immigrant Point

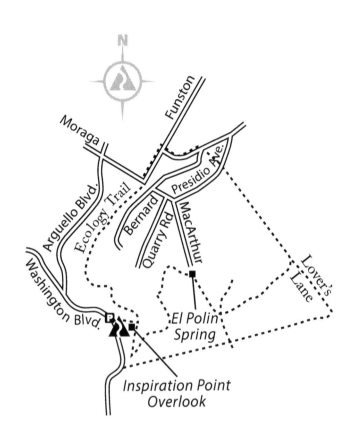

THE PRESIDIO

ECOLOGY LOOP TRAIL

2 miles round trip

The Presidio, a military post turned parkland, occupies some 1,500 acres of real estate in one of America's most desirable cities. Best place to begin a hiking tour of the Presidio is near Inspiration Point on Ecology Trail. This loop trail explores architecture and military history and also offers a nice walk in the woods.

Be sure to stop at the state-of-the-art William Penn Mott, Jr. Presidio Visitor Center, located in the heart of the park next to the Presidio Transit Center. Operated by the National Park Service, the Presidio Trust, and the Golden Gate National Parks Conservancy, the visitor center offers lively videos and interactive exhibits to tell the stories of the Presidio's rich history and natural setting.

Interpretive displays highlight the park's regions including the Main Post and its array of cultural and historical sites; Crissy Field (and other recreational areas); the "Southern Wild" and its nature exploration opportunities and of course the Golden Gate Bridge and its iconic views. The gift shop offers a quality array of books, apparel, merchandise and picnic supplies.

After a century and a half of use, the U.S. Army transferred ownership of San Francisco's historic Presidio to the National Park Service in 1994. Buildings have been restored, and landscapes, too, including hiking trails, wildlife habitat and the unique urban forest. The Presidio hosts an astonishing number (280 species) of native plants More than 200 species of birds have been counted in the urban preserve.

Several periods of architecture are represented in the Presidio, ranging from red brick barracks, circa 1895, built in the Georgian style, to a Spanish Revival-style theater. Some experts rate the Victorian-era officers' homes along Funston Ave. among the best examples of that period in San Francisco.

Environmentally conscious Army Major W.A. Jones is credited with initiating a forestry program in the 1880s that transformed the forlorn, windswept sand dunes into the wooded preserve it is today. Thousands of trees were planted: acacia, eucalyptus, Monterey pine, redwood, madrone, and many more.

Once landscaped, the Presidio proved to be a highly desirable stateside location for a soldier's assignment. Although the base was used mainly as a medical facility and administration center, during

World War II its coastal batteries were activated in order to defend the Golden Gate Bridge against possible enemy attack.

DIRECTIONS: From the Presidio's Arguello Gate entrance, just north of Arguello Blvd. and Jackson St., drive a few hundred yards to the paved parking area on the right, at Inspiration Point. The trailhead is on the east side.

THE HIKE: From the parking area, descend wooden steps and turn left to join Ecology Trail, a wide dirt trail. After passing Inspiration Point itself, make a gradual descent through groves of Monterey pine and eucalyptus.

Ahead lie the buildings of Main Post, holding the Presidio's oldest structures, dating back to 1861.

Now the path is paved. Pass Pershing Hall—a bachelor officers' quarters, and continue along the sidewalk on Funston Ave.

Turn right at Presidio Ave. and continue over a footbridge. Cross MacArthur and continue onto paved Lovers' Lane, a favorite of romantic walkers since the 1860s when it was used by off-duty soldiers to walk into town to meet their sweethearts.

A gradual uphill grade leads near the historic site of El Polin Springs, used by Spanish soldiers more than 200 years ago. More than two dozen varieties of trees can be seen along the trail. Ascend to the base of Inspiration Point, and follow your route back to the parking lot.

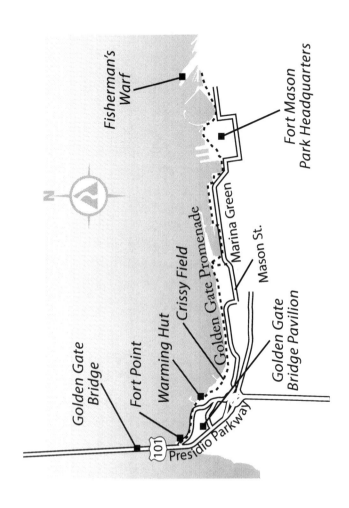

Fisherman's Warf

Fort Mason Park Headquarters

Golden Gate Promenade

Crissy Field

Warming Hut

Fort Point

Golden Gate Bridge

Marina Green

Mason St.

Golden Gate Bridge Pavilion

Presidio Parkway

101

GOLDEN GATE PROMENADE

From Fort Mason to Golden Gate Bridge is 8 miles round trip; along Crissy Field is 2 to 3 miles round trip

Golden Gate Promenade is San Francisco's best, most popular and most scenic bayshore walk. Along the 4-mile path extending from Aquatic Park to Golden Gate Bridge is a rich diversity of historical, architectural and cultural attractions complemented by sandy beaches, a vast waterfront green, and inspiring vistas of the Golden Gate Bridge.

At the dawn of the 21st century, a spectacular eco-transformation occurred on the once degraded Crissy Field shoreline, used by the U.S. Army as an airfield from 1921 until 1936. The now rehabbed coastal environs include a restored salt marsh, repurposed buildings and a network of walking and biking paths.

Fort Mason (a great walk itself) is the north shore's culture capital. Piers and warehouses of Fort Mason Center host theater performances, seminars and recreational activities. GGNRA headquarters is located in a white three-story building.

DIRECTIONS: Fort Mason and parking lots maintained by the Golden Gate National Recreation Area are free. Enter Fort Mason at Franklin and Bay Streets. If you happen to snag a parking space near Fisherman's Wharf, keep it; begin walking the promenade from there.

THE HIKE: From Fort Mason take the paved pathway along the bayshore Sunbathers enjoy snuggling into the hollows of grassy Marina Green to get out of the wind, which is considerable!

At St. Francis Yacht Harbor, note the seawall, which offers a great stroll; at its end, is a wave organ, which (when the tide is right) serenades with the sounds of San Francisco Bay. The promenade joins Marina Boulevard for a time then leads to the Crissy Field Center (providing environmental education for youth and leadership training) and Warming Hut Bookstore and Café.

Golden Gate National Parklands extends along restored Crissy Field Marsh, then along wide Crissy Field itself. Check out the Greater Farallones National Marine Sanctuary Visitor Center to learn about the islands that lie outside the Golden Gate.

On the field's inland side, former airplane hangars have been repurposed for indoor recreation: trampolines, climbing walls, yoga studios. At the west end of Crissy Field, look for West Bluff Picnic Area, the warm and welcoming Warming Hut (café and gift shop), and fishing pier (Torpedo Wharf).

Continue toward Fort Point then join the short pathway ascending to Battery East, once part of the city's coastal defense system. Head toward the Bridge on Bay Trail, then make an easy ascent to Golden Gate Bridge Pavilion, which offers great vistas, info about the bridge, a retail store and visitor center.

Back at Fort Mason, consider walking east to Aquatic Park (benches, lawns, sandy beach). Near the park stands, well, floats, San Francisco Maritime National Historic Park and its intriguing collection of historic ships. The maritime museum is housed in a onetime 1930s' bathhouse, built in the form of a luxury ocean liner.

Don't miss—not that you could—Fisherman's Wharf, San Francisco's most popular destination, known for its delicious seafood, historic waterfront and grand views of San Francisco Bay.

Iconic Fisherman's Wharf, a must-visit.

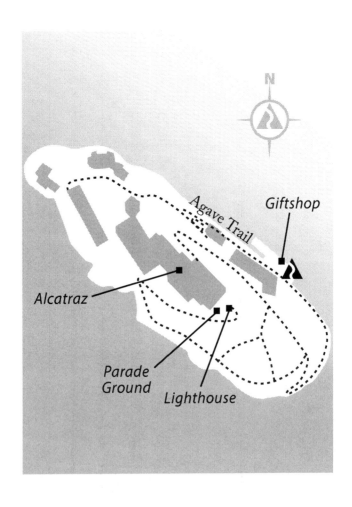

ALCATRAZ ISLAND

AGAVE TRAIL

1 mile round trip including prison tour

Once the island was populated with the likes of
Al "Scarface" Capone, George "Machine Gun" Kelly
and a couple hundred more incorrigibles. Now the
isle's most distinguished residents are the black-
crowned night heron, double-crested cormorant and
a few thousand Western gulls.

The birds have taken over Alcatraz. Allowing the
birds to re-colonize "The Rock" is part of a park service program to restore some semblance of the natural world on an island long synonymous with one of
America's most infamous maximum security prisons.

The Pacific Coast's first lighthouse was installed
on the island in 1854. Alcatraz later served as a
military prison. From 1934 to 1963, The Rock im-
prisoned some of America's most infamous "public
enemies." Alcatraz became part of the GGNRA,

opened to the public in 1973, and has been a popular attraction ever since.

Visitors can tour the prison's cell house with the help of a 45-minute audio tour that features the voices of inmates and guards. Ranger-led walk topics include Famous Inmates, Escapes and Hollywood's Rock. Note: The hike from the boat dock to the cell house is the equivalent of climbing a 13-story building.

Agave Trail takes its name from the island's dense population of the spiny succulent, strategically planted during the isle's prison era to discourage would-be rescuers from coming ashore. The trail leads near tide pools and a sea lion haul-out and offers great views of flocks of sea birds.

Autumn is the best time for a visit. Agave Trail is open only from mid-September through January. The trail is closed the balance of the year in order to protect the nesting sites of the western gull and other fowl. The fall season typically offers the clearest Bay views, as well as relief from the hordes of summer visitors.

Movie fans might recognize locations from Clint Eastwood's *Escape from Alcatraz* and *The Rock,* the latter a 1996 action thriller starring Sean Connery and Nicholas Cage as unlikely heroes who attempt to thwart terrorists who've taken over Alcatraz and are threatening San Francisco with chemical weapons.

DIRECTIONS: Alcatraz Island is accessible by ferry (Alcatraz Cruises), which depart from Pier 33, located on The Embarcadero near Bay Street. Park in one of the many fee lots nearby. Advance Reservations are suggested during summer, weekends and holidays in particular.

Signed Agave Trail begins just south of the ferry dock at an inviting picnic ground.

THE HIKE: The path meanders past eucalyptus (favored by nesting black-crowned night herons) and across a hillside spiked with the trail's namesake agave.

The trail descends toward the water and, at low tide, some intriguing tide pools, then ascends sandstone steps to serve up vistas of the Bay Bridge, Treasure Island and metro San Francisco.

Back up top is a parade ground hewn out of solid rock by military prisoners of the 1870s. Agave Trail passes the ruins of a guardhouse and junctions the main trail to the cellblock. Hikers can continue to the isle's old lighthouse.

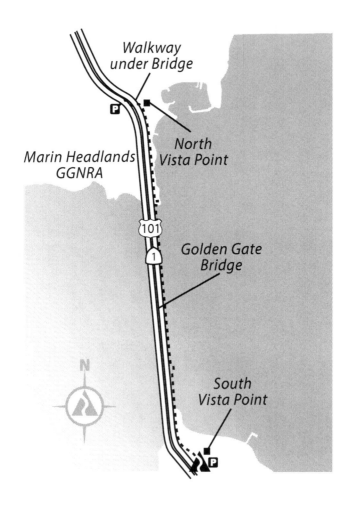

Walkway under Bridge

Marin Headlands GGNRA

North Vista Point

101

1

Golden Gate Bridge

N

South Vista Point

GOLDEN GATE BRIDGE

**Across the Golden Gate from Fort Point to Vista Point is
3 miles round trip**

It's one of the world's engineering marvels, the
proud emblem of a proud city, and "The Bridge at
the End of the Continent." The Golden Gate is all of
this—and a great walk: a must-do, once-in-a-lifetime
adventure.

Native Californian that I am, I knew from an
early age that you could—and should—walk across
the Golden Gate Bridge. A great number of fellow
hikers, though, many of them well traveled, from
across the U.S. and around the world, are unaware
that the bridge is walkable.

For all its utilitarian value, the bridge is an artistic
triumph. How many set-in-San Francisco movies and
television shows have opened with an establishing
shot of the bridge? A lot!

The technically inclined revel in the bridge's vital
statistics: its 8,981-foot length, cables that support 200

million pounds, twin towers the height of 65-story buildings. And just imagine the number of gallons of International Orange paint required to cover 10 million square feet of bridge! The bridge spans 400 square miles of San Francisco Bay, which contains 90 percent of California's remaining coastal wetlands.

While the walk across the bridge is unique, and clear-day views grand, the trip can also be wearing on the nerves. A bone-chilling wind often buffets bridge walkers, and traffic vibrating the bridge also seems to vibrate one's very being. Those afraid of heights should walk near the traffic lanes rather than by the bridge rails.

You can begin from Fort Point, a huge Civil War-era structure built of red brick. From 1933 to 1937, the fort was the coordinating center for the bridge construction. After touring the fort, walk up a road to the viewpoint.

Check out the statue of visionary engineer Joseph Strauss, who persuaded a doubting populace to build the bridge. Learn more about the bridge at the Golden Gate Bridge Welcome Center, located in the visitor plaza at the span's southern end. Check out the landmark Round House Café, a diner in a circular art deco building overlooking the Golden Gate Bridge. It originally opened in 1938, one year after the bridge was completed. The Roundhouse Gift Center offers unique Bridge-themed gifts and apparel.

DIRECTIONS: Parking is available in the parking lot on the southeast side of the bridge. Northbound travelers should take the last San Francisco exit off Highway 101. Warning: First-time visitors often miss the viewpoint parking area just south of the toll plaza and before they know it, end up in Sausalito. Fort Point's parking lot is a good place to park, as are other lots along the bay.

THE HIKE: Walk along the bridge's east sidewalk and enjoy great views of Fort Point located far below. Pause to watch the ship traffic: yachts, tankers, tug boats, ferries, passenger liners, and enormous container cargo vessels.

The bridge's second high tower marks the beginning of Marin County. Splendorous clear-day views include the cities of the East Bay, the bold headlands of Marin, Alcatraz and Angel islands and the San Francisco skyline.

Vista Point is the end of your bridge walk. Here you'll witness tourists from around the world photographing each other and proclaiming their admiration for the Golden Gate in a dozen languages.

Get high above Tennessee Valley. Great hike!

EVERY TRAIL TELLS A STORY.

II

MARIN HEADLANDS

HIKE ON.

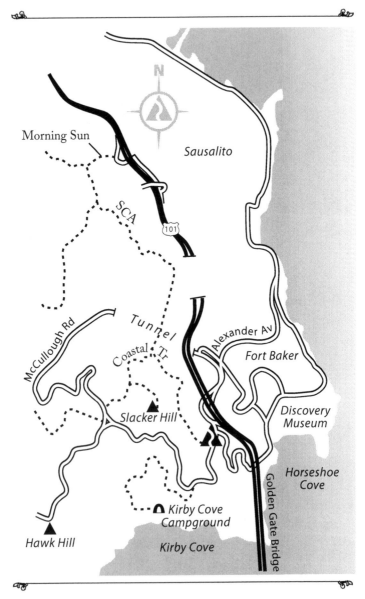

Morning Sun

N

Sausalito

SCA

101

McCullough Rd

Tunnel Tr

Coastal Tr

Alexander Av

Fort Baker

Slacker Hill

Discovery Museum

Horseshoe Cove

Golden Gate Bridge

Kirby Cove Campground

Hawk Hill

Kirby Cove

TheTrailmaster.com

SLACKER HILL

From GG Bridge North Tower Parking to Slacker Hill via Coastal Trail is 3.2 miles round trip with 600-foot elevation gain; from Conzelman Road to Slacker Hill is 1-mile round trip with 300-foot gain

The short hikes to Slacker Hill yield a big reward: a superb 360-degree panoramic vista of the Golden Gate Bridge, San Francisco Bay and Marin Headlands.

While its trailheads are close to popular bridge viewpoints, Slacker Hill itself is a destination off the tourist track and something of a Bay Area insider's hike. You can't be a slacker—that is to say, one who avoids work or effort—to get to the top of this hill. Getting to the trailhead takes a bit of doing and it's best to plan your outings for times of low traffic.

You have two options to hike Slacker Hill: a half-mile ascent from Conzelman Road or a longer route that begins from a trailhead near the Golden Gate Bridge. If you want to factor trailhead parking into your choice of hikes, know that the lot by the bridge holds nearly 50 vehicles, the one off Conzelman Road has a mere 10 parking spaces.

The short way to the top of Slacker Hill can be a memorable sunset hike. Just don't get so enraptured by watching the day star sink into the Pacific that you fail to get down by dark.

You'll follow the narrow trail lined with lizard tail and monkeyflower for a few hundred feet, cross the road and join Coastal Trail (a fire road) at a gate.

Coastal Trail climbs through coastal scrub community that seems to have a longer-than-usual wildflower season—perhaps because of the fog drip. After a 0.25-mile ascent, you'll reach a junction and go right. Another 0.25-mile climb takes you to the flat summit of Slacker Hill.

A longer, but not particularly difficult way to the top of Slacker Hill is by way of Coastal Trail, which leads north from the bridge 1.3 miles to a junction with SCA Trail. Coastal Trail then bends west and intersects the short length of fire road leading up to Slacker Hill.

SCA Trail offers you a couple attractive hiking options. The well-built, well maintained trail hewed into the coastal slopes was named for the Student Conservation Association, which organizes young people for hands on work on public lands—including the Golden Gate National Parks. When the cloud curtain parts and the sun shines over the bay, this trail offers the hiker a unique perspective from the north side of the Golden Gate Bridge.

From its junction with Coastal Trail, SCA Trail leads over the Bunker Road Tunnel to meet Rodeo Valley Trail that, in turn, takes you to Rodeo Lagoon and Rodeo Beach. Another option is to continue on SCA Trail to Morning Sun Trail, which offers great bay views as it switchbacks down to Sausalito.

DIRECTIONS: (from the bridge) Start the longer jaunt to Hawk Hill at the Golden Gate Bridge North Tower parking lot. (from Conzelman Road) Northbound on Highway 101, take the first exit past the viewpoint—Alexander Avenue. Bear left on Alexander, which leads under the highway. Turn right on Conzelman Road to an intersection (rotary) with McCullough Road, where you'll turn right into the parking lot.

The suspension bridge is one of the fun highlights of the hike to Point Bonita Lighthouse.

POINT BONITA LIGHTHOUSE

To Lighthouse is 1-mile round trip

Built in 1855 to guide ships through the dangerous Golden Gate Straits, Point Bonita Lighthouse is a curious sight-to-see with great views of San Francisco. The paved trail passes through a long tunnel and across a long, high wooden suspension bridge. Fun!

The lighthouse is open Sundays and Mondays from 12:30 pm to 3:30 pm. Lines to get into the lighthouse can be long. Arrive well before 3:30 pm to ensure you are able to cross the suspension bridge.

DIRECTIONS: Drive north across the Golden Gate Bridge, exit on Alexander Avenue (just beyond the Vista Point), go 0.2 miles to Bunker Road, and proceed to the one-way Baker-Barry Tunnel, controlled by a stoplight. Travel through the tunnel and after 2 miles turn left onto Field Road. Continue 0.6 mile past the Visitor Center to the Point Bonita Parking Lot.

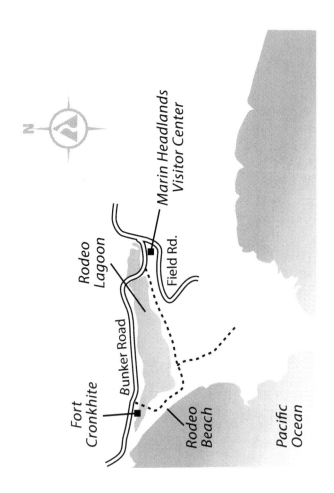

Rodeo Lagoon

Marin Headlands Visitor Center

Field Rd.

Rodeo Beach

Bunker Road

Fort Cronkhite

Pacific Ocean

N

RODEO LAGOON

RODEO LAGOON LOOP TRAIL

To Rodeo Beach is 1.5 miles round trip

Rodeo Valley is the mother of all trailheads for the Marin Headlands, the jump-off place for explorations of beaches, military history and the bold beauty of the headlands themselves. A super-sized parking area off Bunker Road offers easy access to the valley's trails.

Sweeping grasslands, pebbly beaches, and ridgetops with dramatic vistas beckon the hiker. To learn more about Marin's military past and its considerable environmental attractions, stop at the Marin Headlands Visitor Center.

The visitor center is housed in what was once the Fort Barry Chapel, an interdenominational gathering place built in 1941 that held services for servicemen preparing to go to war. The center offers displays interpreting the area's history from the native Coast Miwok era to modern times, as well as a fine little gift shop and bookstore.

Rodeo Lagoon Trail is the easiest of introductions to the headlands; in fact, it's about the only flat trail around. Gaze up at the headlands back of the visitor center. Kind of hilly, huh?

On the way to Rodeo Beach, the trail skirts the mostly freshwater lagoon, home to flotillas of ducks, as well as pelicans, egrets, herons and kingfishers. The pebbly, often windy beach is not a beach for sunbathing but is a favorite of surfers and a treat for beach hikers who marvel at the dark sand beach and the scattered red and green pebbles (chert). Rodeo Beach's mineral make-up is one-of-a-kind; no other beach in California has this kind of look and composition.

The cliffs above the beach offer a fine vantage point for a look at the harbor seals and sea lions swimming in the surf and resting on the rocks. Strong currents and cold water discourage swimmers and all but the boldest surfers.

While something in our hikers' genes attracts us to loop trails, you might want to pass on the return leg of the Rodeo Lagoon Loop; in The Trailmaster's view, it travels too close to Bunker Road for hiking pleasure.

DIRECTIONS: From Highway 101 northbound, just north of the Golden Gate Bridge, exit on Alexander Avenue. Turn left and go under 101, then briefly back-track south to Conzelman Road. Bear right and drive a mile to junction McCullough Road. Turn right and proceed 0.8 mile to Bunker Road.

Turn left and drive 2 miles to the parking area for the Marin Headlands Visitor Center.

Join signed Lagoon Trail on the west side of the parking lot.

THE HIKE: The wide gravel path meanders westward alongside the lagoon, which is fringed with cattails and thickets of willows. Picnic tables near the wetland offer a place to relax.

You soon reach the beach, a narrow barrier that separates the lagoon from the Pacific. Only in winter do storm waves surge over this beach into the lagoon. The resultant mix of saltwater-freshwater is an ideal habitat for many plants and birds.

Follow the hiking trail a bit up the bluffs to admire the coast and rock islands. Largest of the rock isles is guano-crested Bird Island, occupied by a multitude of gulls and brown pelicans.

Picture perfect: Resident pelican and the peaceful waters of Rodeo Lagoon.

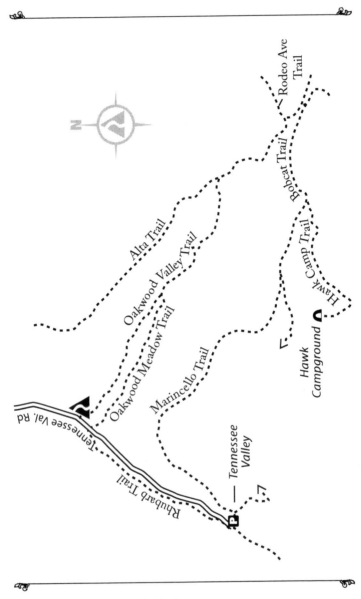

Alta Trail

Oakwood Valley Trail

Oakwood Meadow Trail

Marincello Trail

Tennessee Val. Rd

Rhubarb Trail

Bobcat Trail

Rodeo Ave Trail

Hawk Camp Trail

Hawk Campground

Tennessee Valley

N

OAKWOOD VALLEY

Loop via Oakwood Valley and Oakwood Meadow Trail is 1.3 miles round trip; loop via Oakwood Valley, Alta, Bobcat, Rhubarb Trails is 5 miles round trip with 700-foot elevation gain

Oakwood Valley, overlooked by nearly everyone on their way to the nearby Tennessee Valley Trailhead, is a gem of a short walk or an inspiring start for longer explorations across the Marin Headlands. Considering the valley's trailhead is but a 15-minute drive from the Golden Gate Bridge, the trail offers more peace and solitude than you might imagine.

Oakwood Valley Trail, a kid-friendly, stroller-friendly fire road, meets up with Oakwood Meadow Trail to make a near-loop. The route leads through groves of bay laurel and eucalyptus, the latter planted by early residents of Oakwood Valley to mark property boundaries and serve as windbreaks.

Depending on your time and inclination, you can fashion a half-dozen different loops or out-and backs from Oakwood Valley trailhead. One of my favorites is a 5-mile loop that pops out on a ridge for great San Francisco Bay views, then drops down to Tennessee Valley Trailhead. A short jaunt on pleasant and shady Rhubarb Trail completes the loop.

DIRECTIONS: From Highway 1 in Marin City, turn left on Tennessee Valley Road and travel 0.9 mile to the signed trailhead at a white metal gate. Snag one of the few parking spaces near the trailhead or park on the right side of the road nearby.

THE HIKE: Stroll the wide trail through a mixed woodland of eucalyptus and toyon, and past a grassy meadow. After an easy 0.6 mile, you'll reach a pond. Take a seat on the bench and look for and listen for the (threatened) California red-legged frog. To complete the short loop, cross the creek on a footbridge and head back on Oak Valley Trail.

Oakwood Valley Trail steepens, your ascent assisted by several sets of steps. Reward for the climb to meet Alta Trail is a bird's eye view: Sausalito and its multitude of watercraft, across Richardson Bay to Tiburon, and an unusual angle on Angel Island.

Alta Trail leads 0.4 mile to a junction with Rodeo Avenue Trail on the left. Hike another 0.1 mile to Bobcat Trail on your right. Descend steeply, regain lost elevation, and pass the connector trail leading 0.7 mile to Hawk Camp, GGNRA's most remote camp (3 sites, reservations only), perched high above Gerbode Valley in a clump of pine trees.

After 0.8 mile on Bobcat Trail, pass a junction with Miwok Trail, and continue on Marincello Trail. Enjoy over-the-shoulder views of the bay and Richmond-San Rafael Bridge. After a mile, descend past a line of cypress to Tennessee Valley Trailhead. Across the road, look for

Rhubarb Trail and join the heavily shaded path as it parallels a creek and Tennessee Valley Road. On the weekends it can be crowded on the narrow trail—but it's a way better way to return to the trailhead than walking along the road.

Coyotes are frequently sighted in this part of the GGNRA.

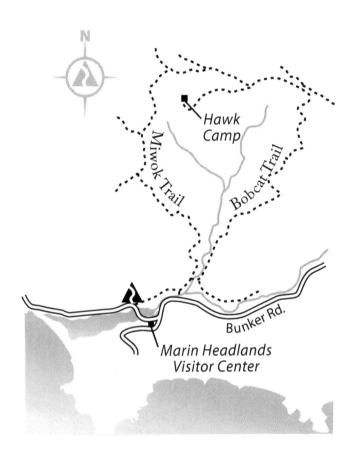

N

Hawk
Camp

Miwok Trail

Bobcat Trail

Bunker Rd.

Marin Headlands
Visitor Center

Marin Headlands

Miwok, Bobcat Trails

Loop around Gerbode Valley is 6.8 miles round trip with 800-foot elevation gain

Just a mile back from the coast, northeast of Rodeo Valley, lies a land that many hikers adjudge to be GGNRA's wildest. Lovely Gerbode Valley is the centerpiece of the Marin Headlands backcountry.

In the mid-1960s, developers intended to construct enough houses, stores and roads to support a city of 18,000 people on this wildland. Thanks to the efforts of conservationists, the land passed from military to National Park Service administration and spared from development.

From the ridgetops above the valley, the hiker gains great views of the bay from Tiburon to the Golden Gate Bridge towers, as well as to the north of mighty Mt. Tam.

Keep an eye on the sky for raptors, particularly during the fall migration when the hawks and their aerial acrobatics are an awesome sight. Also look for ravens and turkey vultures.

A fine network of trails explores the Marin Headlands. For a fine circle tour, take Miwok Trail on a mellow climb to the ridgeline, then descend via Bobcat Trail.

Check out the Marin Headlands Visitor Center, offering maps, information and an eclectic collection of exhibits about the native Miwok, Spanish days, the American military and the area's many natural attractions.

DIRECTIONS: From Highway 101 northbound, just north of the Golden Gate Bridge, exit on Alexander Avenue. Head north 0.2 mile, turn left on Bunker Road and soon reach a stoplight at the mouth of a one-way-at-a-time tunnel. About 2.7 miles from the highway, look for the signed turnoff to the Marin Headlands on the left; at this bend in the road, turn right into the lot and park near signed Miwok Trail, which begins by a warehouse.

THE HIKE: Miwok Trail gets off to kind of a pedestrian start, wide and flat for 0.5 mile to its meeting with a very short connector trail coming in from the right that links to Bobcat Trail. Begin a shade-less, 1.1 mile ascent to the eastern end of Wolf Ridge. Enjoy vistas of Mt. Tam and the Pacific Ocean and pass junctions with Wolf Ridge Trail and Old Springs Trail.

Greetings Earthlings. You might think you hiked into an old sci-fi flick when you see Vortac, an aircraft navigational aid.

Next step toward a scene out of an old science fiction flick: a white space capsule-like metal cone pointed skyward from the 1,041-foot high point on the ridge between Gerbode and Tennessee valleys. Vortac is a FAA directional homing device for aircraft.

Descend to a junction, part company with Miwok Trail, and join east-trending Bobcat Trail which leads 0.3 mile to intersect the road that travels to walk-in Hawk Camp.

Pass more connector trails leading to Alta and Rodeo Valley trails as Bobcat Trail swings south, makes a mellow descent into Gerbode Valley and offers views of Highway 101, Sausalito and Richardson Bay. Reach the signed connector trail and rejoin Miwok Trail for the return to the trailhead.

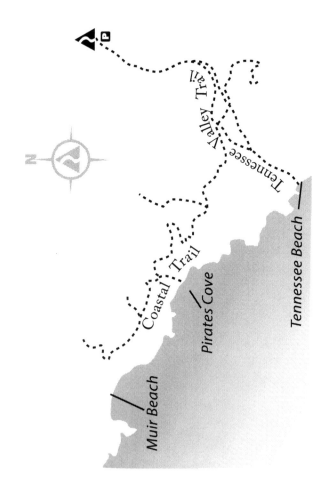

TENNESSEE VALLEY

From Tennessee Valley to Tennessee Cove is 4 miles round trip; to Muir Beach is 9 miles round trip with 800-foot elevation gain

It was a dark and stormy night...when the side-wheel steamship *Tennessee* with 600 passengers aboard, overshot the Golden Gate and ran aground off this isolated Marin County cove. Fortunately no lives were lost on that foggy night of March 6, 1853. The vessel is remembered by a point, a cove, a valley and a beach.

Located only a few miles north of San Francisco, Tennessee Valley, walled in by high ridges, seems quite isolated from the world. (However, this is a very popular trailhead offering many hiking options!) The walk through Tennessee Valley to Tennessee Beach is suitable for the whole family. More intrepid hikers will join Coastal Trail for an up-and-down journey to Muir Beach.

DIRECTIONS: From Highway 101 north of the Golden Gate Bridge, take the Highway 1 of-framp. Follow the highway a half-mile, turn left on

Tennessee Valley Road, and follow this road to the trailhead and parking area.

THE HIKE: Tennessee Valley Trail begins as a paved road (farther on it becomes gravel, farther still it becomes a footpath.) The route descends moderately alongside a willow-and eucalyptus-lined creek. The American kestrel and a variety of hawk patrol the skies above the valley.

After 0.25 mile, pass the trail to Haypress Trail Camp and soon thereafter, Fox Trail, both of which veer to the northwest (right). The road reaches a private residence at the 0.7-mile mark and turns to dirt.

A mile out, take the left-forking trail, which is a seasonal (hikers only) footpath that wends its way around a willow-lined marshy area. If this path looks like it's too wet for easy travel, continue with the drier and higher main Tennessee Valley Trail. The main path passes a pine-shaded pit toilet and intersects Coastal Trail.

The seasonal footpath and the main Tennessee Valley Trail reunite about 0.5 mile from Tennessee Cove. Continue to the western end of the marshland and follow the creek to Tennessee Beach.

A narrow path ascends stairs and the steep slopes north of the beach to a vista point adjacent to a onetime military bunker. Explore the 300-yard long beach and retrace your steps on the main Tennessee Valley Trail this time forking left and ascending to meet Coastal Trail.

Ascend north on Coastal Trail to the top of a knoll, where the trail splits into a fire road that turns inland and a footpath that continues closer to the coast. I highly recommend the footpath way. Coastal Trail (the footpath) flattens out a bit, then descends to Pirate's Cove. The trail marches up and down the coastal bluffs, and passes a junction with Coyote Ridge Trail. You'll get grand views of Muir Beach and Green Gulch. From this junction, descend rather steeply to Muir Beach, a wide, semi-circular strand enclosed by a forested cove, and featuring newly improved visitor facilities. From the beach, you can walk a dirt road 0.75 mile to the Pelican Inn, an authentic-looking English pub that serves traditional pub fare and a great selection of ales.

California Coastal Trail or Pacific Coast Trail: by whatever name this path between Tennessee Beach and Muir Beach is stunning.

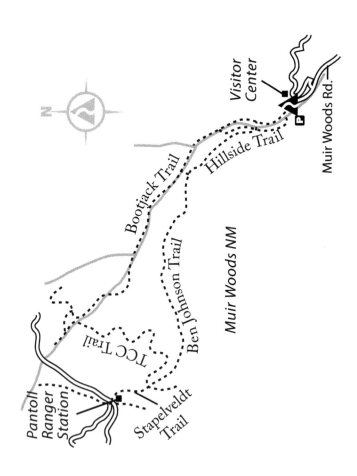

Visitor Center

Muir Woods Rd.

Bootjack Trail

Hillside Trail

Ben Johnson Trail

Muir Woods NM

TCC Trail

Pantoll Ranger Station

Stapelveldt Trail

N

TheTrailmaster.com

Muir Woods
National Monument

2-mile loop and 6-mile loop with 1,000-foot elevation gain

Muir Woods draws an international crowd. While hiking the trails, expect to hear praise of the tall trees in a half-dozen languages, though something about these cathedrals of redwoods lowers the volume on even the most effusive visitors.

"This is the best tree-lover's monument that could possibly be found in all the forests of the world," wrote John Muir upon learning a redwood preserve was dedicated in his name. "You have done me great honor and I am proud of it."

Most of the many, many visitors a year who walk in Muir Woods would agree with the great naturalist. The national monument is a must-see for visitors from around the state and around the world.

(Tips to beat the crowds: Arrive early [before 9 a.m.] or late [after 5 p.m.], and visit on weekdays.)

The main, nearly flat trail along Redwood Creek is paved. Bridges over Redwood Creek enable the hiker to make several loops. Muir Woods is linked by trail to Mt. Tamalpais State Park; this hike is a grand tour of the redwoods and a Trailmaster favorite.

DIRECTIONS: Muir Woods is only 12 miles from the Golden Gate Bridge. From Highway 101 northbound to Mill Valley, take the Highway 1/Stinson Beach exit and join Shoreline Highway (1). Head west 2.7 miles to Panoramic Highway, turn right and drive 0.8 mile to Muir Woods Road. Turn left and proceed 1.6 miles to the main parking area for Muir Woods National Monument on your right. A second lot is located about 100 yards southeast.

Parking and shuttle reservations are now required to visit Muir Woods. To book this trip, visit GoMuirWoods.com or call 1-800-410-2419. Heads-up: There's poor or no cell service in or around Muir Woods National Monument. Download your parking reservation or shuttle ticket in advance.

THE HIKE: Pay the entry fee and join the paved, well-traveled trail along Redwood Creek. Pass the visitor center, café and gift shop on the right and Bridge 1 over Redwood Creek on your left. A nature trail with numbered stops and keyed to a park brochure begins at Bridge 2.

Continue along the main trail to Bridge 3 and Cathedral Grove. At a junction with right-forking Fern

Creek Trail, step off the main trail to visit William Kent Memorial Tree a sky-scraping 273-foot high Douglas fir (surprise!), tallest tree in Muir Woods.

For a longer loop, at Bridge 4 join Bootjack Trail and continue along Redwood Creek. The footpath ascends more steeply amidst ferns and occasional big-leaf maple, leaves the creek then returns to it. The path climbs aggressively to a spectacular footbridge over Redwood Creek (Photo op!) ascends fairly steeply to diminutive Van Wyck Meadow and intersects signed TCC Trail, 2.3 miles from the trailhead.

Bear left on TCC Trail and enjoy a mellow, fairly flat 1.3-mile amble through the woods to a meeting with Stapelveldt Trail. Make two left turns to join, and stay on Stapelveldt Trail and hike 0.5 mile to a signed intersection with Ben Johnson Trail.

Join this path and descend a mile to meet Hillside Trail, which leads to Bohemian Grove, and continue on this lightly traveled path 0.8 mile to Bridge 1. Cross the bridge to Main Trail at a point near the visitor center, café, gift shop and park entrance.

John Muir, made of wood, in Muir Woods.

Hike to Mori Point, a national parkland gem on the San Mateo coast.

EVERY TRAIL TELLS A STORY.

III

THE PENINSULA

HIKE ON.

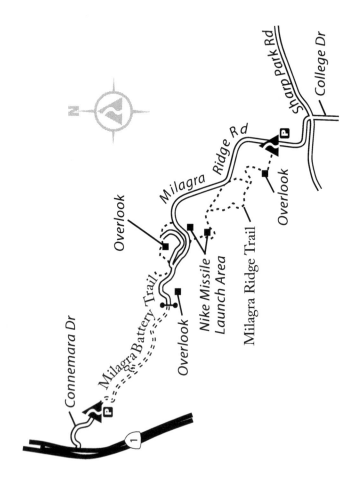

Connemara Dr

Milagra Battery Trail

Overlook

Nike Missile Launch Area

Milagra Ridge Trail

Overlook

Milagra Ridge Rd

Overlook

Sharp Park Rd

College Dr

N

1

MILAGRA RIDGE

MILAGRA RIDGE, MILAGRA BATTERY TRAILS

**From College Avenue to summit via Milagra Ridge Trail
is 1.5 miles round trip with 100-foot elevation gain; from
Connemara Avenue to summit via Milagra Battery Trail
is 1.4 miles round trip with 470-foot elevation gain**

In a word, this hike is a breeze.

The strong winds that whisk over Milagra Ridge
and buffet hikers call to mind the old phrase "hold
onto your hat," but if it's really windy that will be an
impossible task. Sometimes it's so windy, you can't
even hold a conversation with your fellow hikers!

The northwest-southeast trending ridge angles
steeply downward toward Pacifica and the Pacific
Ocean. On clear days (savor them in this often-foggy
locale), ocean views are fantastic. Milagra's open ridge
offers a feeling of scale and expansiveness far greater
than this park unit's size (275 acres) might suggest.

Milagra was once an even more prominent ridge,
but its summit was flattened in the 1950s by the
military during the Cold War in order to install a Nike

missile site. The surface-to-air missiles were intended to defend San Francisco from enemy aircraft. After buildings were demolished and launch elevators buried, Milagra Ridge became part of GGNRA in 1987.

Milagra Ridge is crucial habitat for the rare Mission blue and San Bruno elfin butterflies. These two species survive only in the very particular environment on this ridge, on Sweeney Ridge, and on the slopes of San Bruno Mountain. The National Park Service closely monitors recreational activity to aid survival of the butterflies. One puzzles how a light-as-air butterfly has adapted to an environment noted for such strong winds.

Several endangered plants, including the San Francisco wallflower and coast rockcrest, that cling to life on the ridge's coastal terrace prairie ecosystem. Concern for the butterflies and special flora has led park authorities to close some habitat-disturbing trails on Milagra Ridge and to line others with cable and post fencing. (Please hike only on posted pathways and stay out of habitat recovery areas.)

For 30 years, Milagra Ridge Trail was the only way to go. Completed in 2016, the new Milagra Battery Trail, a wide dirt pathway, gives hikers access to the ridge from Highway 1/Pacifica.

DIRECTIONS: From Highway 1 in Pacifica, follow Sharp Park Road to the east, or from Skyline Boulevard (Highway 35) follow Sharp Park Road to the west. Turn north on College Drive (an entrance to Skyline College) and continue 0.25 mile to roadside parking at the gate.

To Trailhead for Milagra Battery Trail: From Highway 1, about 7 miles south of San Francisco and 2 miles north of Pacifica, take exit 507 toward Monterey Rd. Turn right onto Oceana Blvd and travel 0.1 mile. Turn inland onto Connemara Drive and drive 0.2 mile through a residential area to the trailhead and small parking lot.

THE HIKE: (Milagra Ridge Trail) From the yellow gate, hike along the paved road. The road, part of Bay Area Ridge Trail, heads directly for the ridgetop.

Note: You can also choose to take the dirt Milagra Ridge Trail; the trail and the road meet up in less than 0.5 mile. In fact, the ridge is honeycombed with trails.

Check out the view from multiple Overlooks and head down stairs to check out the former Nike Missile launch area. When the foggy curtain parts, enjoy stunning coastal vistas, as well as views north to Mount Tamalpais and south to Montara Mountain.

Milagra Battery Trail rapidly leaves the residential behind and climbs steeply. Pause on the double-track trail now and then to look down on those great coastal views. Once you reach the ridge, enjoy the breezy and wide open meadows and great vistas from multiple overlooks.

Cold War relic on peaceful Milagra Ridge.

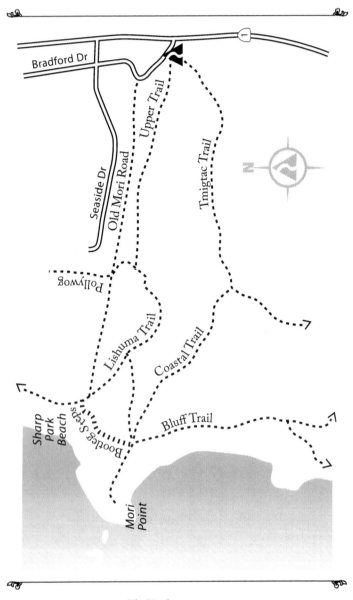

Bradford Dr

Seaside Dr

Old Mori Road

Upper Trail

Tmigtac Trail

N

Pollywog

Lishuma Trail

Coastal Trail

Sharp Park Beach

Boodee Steps

Bluff Trail

Mori Point

TheTrailmaster.com

Mori Point

**Loop to Mori Point via several trails and Old Mori Road is
1.8 miles round trip; to Pacifica Pier is 3.6 miles round trip**

Honeycombed with hiking trails, Mori Point offers a stunning perch (blanketed with wildflowers in
spring) from which to watch a sunset, scan the horizon for migrating whales or take in vistas north to
Pacifica and far beyond.

Bounded by Sharp Beach on the north, tall bluffs
beckoning to be climbed on the south, and frog
ponds and an aesthetically pleasing golf course on
the east, Mori Point seems a whole lot larger on the
ground than it does on the map.

Prior to becoming part of GGNRA, Mori Point
had a long, strange history. The native Aramai (related to the Ohlone) lived here before becoming one of
the first indigenous peoples lured to San Francisco's
Mission Dolores in the early 1800s. During Prohibi-
tion, bootleggers set up a speakeasy and sold liquor
("Bootleggers Steps" is part of the Mori Point trail
system). Adjacent Sharp Park served as a relief camp

for people displaced in the Great Depression of the 1930s and as a WW II POW camp for soldiers from Germany, Italy, and Japan

At the end of the 1971 cult classic film "Harold and Maude," Harold fakes another suicide by sending his hearse off the cliffs. Later in the century, off-road vehicles raced across the headlands and motorcycles tore around a dirt track. Thanks to local residents and conservation groups, who blocked a series of development schemes, Mori Point was purchased and added to the Golden Gate National Parks in the early 2000s.

Working with the National Park Service, community members have rehabbed habitat for the California red-legged frog and the San Francisco garter snake, once considered North America's most endangered reptile. Keep an eye out for a 3-foot-long snake with a turquoise belly red, black, blue, and green stripes.

Mori Point has a well-signed network of short trails that allow you to create a hike of your choosing from 1.5 to 5 miles or so. It's mighty breezy on the point; dress accordingly.

DIRECTIONS: You can only access the Mori Point trailhead from Highway 1 southbound. From Highway 1 in Pacifica, shortly after passing Westport Drive, turn right on Mori Point Road. Park along the road or along Bradford Way.

From Mori Point Road, join signed Upper Mori Trail, lined with purple-hued seaside daisies and hike 0.3 mile southwest to meet Tmigtac Trail. Follow this path to meet Coastal Trail and walk another 0.5 mile to reach Mori Point, which sticks out between two long, sandy beaches. Waves dash in dramatic fashion against the rocks, shooting whitewater skyward.

Take in the grand views of black sand Sharp Beach and Pacifica Pier to the north and tall bluffs to the south. Few hikers venture past the point, but know Bluff Trail and others ascend the bluffs for fabulous coastal views.

From Mori Point double-back and descend exactly 645 feet on the Bootleg Stairs. Warmly greet out-of-breath hikers ascending the stairs. Return via Old Mori Road to complete this loop hike.

For a fun addition to this outing, walk the California Coastal Trail atop the Sea Wall 0.9 mile to Pacifica Pier—or, as a sign whimsically indicates, continue on the CCT 490 miles to the Oregon border! En route, pass frog ponds and Sharp Park Golf Course, considered one of America's great municipal courses.

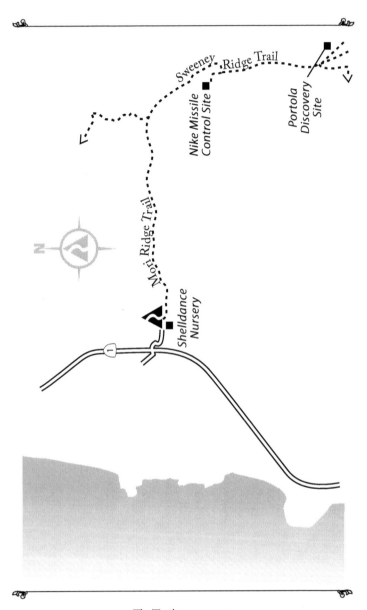

Sweeney Ridge Trail

Moi Ridge Trail

Nike Missile Control Site

Portola Discovery Site

Shelldance Nursery

1

N

TheTrailmaster.com

Mori Ridge

Mori Ridge Trail

To Sweeney Ridge is 4 miles round trip with 900-foot elevation gain

From Pacifica, a short, sweet, and steep climb leads to Mori Ridge, Sweeney Ridge, and panoramic views from San Francisco Bay to the Marin Headlands to Mount Diablo. On the clearest days, spot the Farallon Islands, floating on the western horizon 25 miles away.

The wide multiuse trail, sprinkled with wildflowers in the spring leads to grassy Sweeney Ridge, dotted with blue and purple lupine, orange California poppies, yellow yarrow, white wild radish, purple coastal iris, red Indian paintbrush… The path leads to the far northern end of the Santa Cruz Mountains and to the so-called Bay Discovery Site on Sweeney Ridge. As the story goes, here's where the first Europeans, led by Gaspar de Portolá, laid eyes on San Francisco Bay in 1769.

Strangely enough, Portolá "missed" his intended destination of Monterey Bay and ended up on this obscure ridge above what is now Pacifica. The historical record is now being revised to explain how Portolá, colonists and soldiers arrived sick and malnourished in Ramaytush Ohlone territory, how villagers fed and cared for them, and led them to the ridge overlooking the bay. Keep in mind, for more than two centuries, Europeans had sailed past the narrow, fog-obscured Golden Gate Strait and failed to notice the great natural harbor of San Francisco Bay.

The National Park Service now interprets the Bay Discovery Site like this: "The notion that America was vast and empty, waiting to be discovered and settled by Europeans was based on the pretense that no one of significance was here before. The truth is that indigenous people, with thriving and highly developed cultures, lived across the continent for thousands of years before colonization started."

DIRECTIONS: Trailhead parking is available behind Shelldance Nursery, east of Highway 1, just south of Westport Drive.

THE HIKE: Up you go. During winter and other times of high surf, you can hear the roarrrr of the waves pounding the beach more than a mile away. After some steep climbing, you emerge from the trees and get your first views. To the south, you can't miss Montara Mountain that from this angle seems to rise straight out of the ocean. Below is the city of Pacifica and to the north, lie the neighborhoods on the western coast of San Francisco.

As you climb Mori Ridge, San Francisco's East Bay comes into view, backed by the Oakland-Berkeley Hills and farther back, by mighty Mount Diablo. After a mile of rigorous ascent, the trail levels. Along Sweeney Ridge, learn more strange history from the 1950s Cold War in the form of Nike anti-aircraft missile stations, then hike on until you reach the Discovery Site.

From Mori Ridge and Sweeney Ridge, grand views of the coast south of San Francisco.

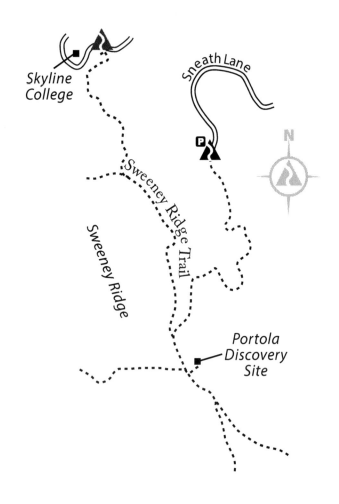

Skyline College

Sneath Lane

Sweeney Ridge Trail

Sweeney Ridge

Portola Discovery Site

N

SWEENEY RIDGE

SWEENEY RIDGE TRAIL

**From Skyline College Trailhead to Discovery Site is
4 miles round trip with 600-foot elevation gain**

Unlike most California coastal locales, San Francisco Bay was discovered by hikers, not sailors. The bay's infamous fog, and its narrow opening had concealed it from passing ships for two centuries when Captain Gaspar de Portola sighted it on November 4, 1769.

The actual discovery site is atop Sweeney Ridge above the town of Pacifica. At first Portola was miffed by his discovery because he realized that his expedition had overshot its intended destination of Monterey Bay. He soon realized, however, that he had discovered one of the world's great natural harbors, and he figured it would be an ideal place for his government to build another presidio.

It was quite a conservation battle to save Sweeney Ridge. The late Congressman Phillip Burton, aided by Bay Area conservationists, succeeded in placing a thousand acres of the ridgetop under protection of the Golden Gate National Recreation Area.

The ridge is often cloaked in morning fog and, in the afternoon, the wind really kicks up. When it's foggy, the coastal scrub and grasslands are bathed in a strange, sharp light. Sweeney Ridge is particularly attractive in spring, when lupine, poppies, cream cups, and goldfields color the slopes.

The view is magnificent: Mt. Tamalpais, Mt. Diablo, the Golden Gate and Farallon Islands, plus dozens of communities clustered around the bay.

Four trails lead to Sweeney Ridge: Baquiano Trail and Mori Ridge Trail lead eastward to Portola's discovery site, while Sneath Lane Trail and Sweeney Ridge Trail climb southward to the ridgetop. I prefer the two southward approaches; they offer more of a feeling of surprise when you climb Sweeney Ridge and behold San Francisco Bay.

DIRECTIONS: To start this hike at Skyline College, take Highway 35 to San Bruno. Turn west on College Drive, following it to the south side of campus. Look for parking area #2. To begin at Sneath Lane, take Highways 280 or 35 to the Sneath Lane exit in San Bruno. Follow the lane westbound to its end at a small parking area. Paved Sneath Lane (closed to vehicle traffic) climbs Sweeney Ridge.

THE HIKE: From Skyline College, join a fire road that rounds a coastal scrub-dotted hill and in

0.75 mile reach the foundations of an old Nike missile site. The trail then drops steeply into a ravine, then begins an equally steep climb out of it.

At the 1-mile mark, Sweeney Ridge Trail is joined by Mori Ridge Trail coming in from the right. Keep to the left with a wide fire road, which travels 0.5 mile to an old radar station that was linked with the Nike missile site. From here, the paved fire road leads a mellow 0.5 mile to the San Francisco Bay Discovery Site.

Return the same way or return via paved Sneath Lane Trail, continuing 0.25 mile beyond the trailhead. Make a left on Riverside Drive, walk another 0.25 mile, go right on the road near the parking area for the county jail, and soon reach parking lot #2 at the Skyline College trailhead.

From this ridge, the Portola expedition "discovered" San Francisco Bay, November 4, 1769.

Reymundo Trail

Mt Redondo Trail

Miramontes Trail

Richards Road

Trail

King Mountain Rd

Crystal Springs Trail

N

PHLEGER ESTATE

CRYSTAL SPRING, RICHARDS ROAD, MIRAMONTE TRAILS

From Huddart County Park to Phleger Estate is 4.2 miles round trip with 200-foot elevation gain; loop via Raymundo and Mt. Redondo Trails is 6.6 miles round trip with 600-foot gain

Woodsy Woodside, one of the Bay Area's priciest and most rustic residential areas, has a park that seems very much in keeping with its neighborhood. You half expect a gated entry or valet parking for the Phleger Estate.

Prominent San Francisco attorney Herman Phleger owned this land of steep canyons and second-growth redwoods at a time when property located 40 miles south of San Francisco was quite rural and removed from city life. Phleger managed to commute by auto over poor roads to offices in the city during the 1930s.

Phleger's 1,227-acre parcel became the southernmost unit of the Golden Gate National Recreation Area in 1995.

The only convenient hiking access to Phleger is by way of adjacent Huddart County Park. Deep and steep ravines, frequently wrapped in fog, support dense stands of redwood. Higher and drier slopes are cloaked in oaks. The estate's main trail traces West Union Creek, which just happens to lie directly on the San Andreas Fault.

DIRECTIONS: From Highway 280 in Woodside, take the Highway 84 (Woodside Road) exit and head west through Woodside for 1.7 miles to Kings Mountain Road. Turn right and travel 1.5 miles to Huddart County Park (entry fee). Park in the first lot, just past the entrance station.

THE HIKE: The wide path lined by a split-rail fence, winds through redwood and madrone as it skirts the Zwierlein Picnic Area. In 0.2 mile you'll join Crystal Spring Trail, sticking with this well-signed path as it passes several trail junctions, then junctions Richards Road. Bear left and a short 0.1 mile ascent up the dirt road will bring you to signed Miramonte Trail and entry to the Phleger Estate.

Join fern-lined Miramonte Trail as it travels alongside Union Creek. Watch for the abundant deer gamboling through the woods and a multitude of banana slugs slithering across the path. An impressive sign, topped by an iron Indian astride a horse, marks the dedication site of the Phleger Estate.

The path continues along bubbling Union Creek before abruptly and briefly turning south and ascending above the creek. Soon the trail changes direction again and heads west to a T-intersection with Mt. Redondo and Raymundo trails. Turn right on Raymundo Trail and begin a counter-clockwise tour of the mountain. Saunter along Union Creek for a bit, then climb above it to another junction marked with a sign and iron Indian.

Unless training for a trek to Nepal, ignore Lonely Trail, which ascends 1,000 feet in elevation to Skyline Boulevard. Instead, bid adieu to Raymundo Trail as it gives way to Mt. Redondo Trail and join this pleasant path as it dips to a trickling creek, crosses it, and descends back to the junction with Miramonte Trail. From this junction, retrace your steps back to the trailhead.

Trail signs here are works-of-art, complete with a Native American on horseback.

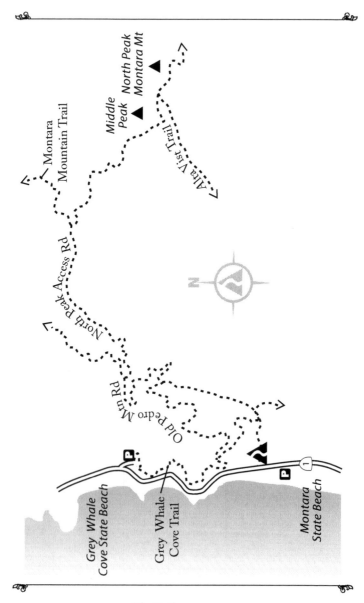

Montara Mountain Trail

North Peak Montara Mt

Middle Peak

North Peak

Alta Vista Trail

Montara Mountain Trail

North Peak Access Rd

Old Pedro Mtn Rd

Grey Whale Cove State Beach

Grey Whale Cove Trail

Montara State Beach

1

TheTrailmaster.com

MONTARA MOUNTAIN

NORTH PEAK ACCESS ROAD TRAIL

To North Peak is 7.8 miles round trip with 1,900-foot elevation gain

Montara Mountain, perched above the San Mateo coast just 10 miles south of San Francisco, offers grand views and wide-open spaces. Reward for the rigorous ascent of the mountain is a panoramic view from Half Moon Bay to the San Francisco skyline to Mt. Diablo.

The slopes of Montara Mountain form the bulk of the McNee Ranch State Park and sprawl into the GGNRA's Rancho Corral de Tierra. Montara Mountain, geologists say, is a 90-million-year-old chunk of granite (largely quartz diorite) that forms the northernmost extension of the Santa Cruz Mountains.

One way to hike up Montara Mountain is to start from adjacent San Pedro Valley County Park, which offers water, restrooms, and a picnic area, ascend on Montara Mountain Trail and descend amidst a mixture of oak, pine, and redwood past Brook Creek Falls.

The hike to the summit from the coast follows wide, dirt, North Peak Access Road all the way to the top. Spring is a splendid time to trek Montara Mountain, known as a "wildflower hike" for its relatively dependable displays of blue-hued ceanothus, blue-eyed grass, Indian paintbrush, lupine and California poppies. And more than a few random blooms!

(BTW what is a great place to hike was long considered an ideal location for a multi-lane highway by the California Department of Transportation. Caltrans suggested building a Highway 1 bypass through the park to replace the existing landslide- prone stretch of highway known as the Devil's Slide that begins about two miles south of Pacifica. Caltrans' plans were fiercely contested by environmentalists!)

For hikers like me who like loop trails, I have good news and bad news. The good news is aptly named Alta Vista Trail, which crosses GGNRA's Rancho Corral de Tierra, offers a way to make a Montara Mountain loop. The bad news is Alta Vista Trail is super-steep, gravelly, and slippery. If you decide to tackle the trail, use it on the ascent to reduce the risk of falling.

DIRECTIONS: To reach the trailhead, travel 6 miles south of Pacifica on(and 0.7 south of Gray Whale Cove State Beach) on Highway 1. Northbound travelers will follow Highway 1 about 0.5 mile north of Montara. Look for a small lot near the signed entry to McNee Ranch State Park. If the lot is full, find parking north and south along the coast side of Highway 1, and at the Montara State Beach lot.

THE HIKE: Signed North Peak Access Road heads east at first, along Martini Creek and amidst a stand of cypress. (In the early going, you might find yourself in the company of other hikers, who are joining the road from Grey Whale Cove Trail and other unnamed pathways.)

About 0.25 from the trailhead, reach the park ranger residence, and the road turns north. The route steepens and continues to travel in the company of cypress. This seems to me a magical length of trail, a soft gold in the morning light, with the misty mountains beckoning you onward.

Old San Pedro Mountain Road splits off to left as North Point Access Road leaves the cypress behind, passes one lone tree at a junction with Grey Whale Trail, and continues its rigorous ascent, bending northeast, then east.

About 3 miles out, Access Road intersects Montara Mountain Trail. From the junction, enjoy views north to San Francisco and Half Moon Bay. Continue southeast to road's end, a microwave tower and weather station. From the summit of Montara Mountain's North Peak, partake of the wonderful views, including Mt. Tamalpais and across the Pacific to the Farallon Islands.

French Trail

Clipper Ridge Trail

Deer Creek Trail

Flat Top Tr

Almeria Trail

Coral Reef

Granada

1

RANCHO CORRAL DE TIERRA

Loop via Clipper Ridge and French Trails is 3.3 miles with 600 foot-elevation gain

Rancho Corral de Tierra, a onetime Mexican land grant dating from 1839, is now part of Golden Gate National Recreation Area. To the Spanish, the ridge and coastline around Half Moon Bay resembled a large natural corral, prompting the name of the rancho, meaning "Corral of the Earth."

One of the largest tracts of undeveloped land on the San Mateo peninsula became national parkland in 2005. Conservationists saved 4,000-plus acres of the old rancho from upscale subdivision complete with ranchettes and a golf course. The National Park Service and partners is restoring the native grasslands and improving habitat for wildlife, including coyotes, bobcats, grey foxes and mountain lions.

A diverse group of farmers—Chinese, Italian, Irish, Portuguese, as well as the original Mexican/Californios—cultivated artichokes and Brussel sprouts. As the story goes, the remote area was also a favorite of notorious Prohibition-era gangsters. Al Capone's brother-in-law owned a roadhouse, where hitmen left the body of a man who ran afoul of the organized crime ring.

The headwaters of four creeks—Denniston, San Vincente, Monterey and Martini—rise from the top of the rancho. These watersheds, along with the coastal scrub and chaparral environments on the slopes above the creeks, nurture a variety of native flora and such rare species as the Montara manzanita, Montara bush lupine and San Francisco wallflower.

Hikers will find rancho trails steeper and more eroded than the usual high quality National Park Service paths. And don't expect parking lots and developed trailheads. Most hikes begin in community neighborhoods and nearly all trail-users are locals. Options include a 3-mile loop via Farmer's Daughter Trail and Spine Ridge Trail in the foothills above Cabrillo Farms in Moss Beach. Quarry Park also offers some short hikes. Hikers be forewarned: lots of mountain bikers in these parts!

The trail system is very much a work-in-progress and the trails crisscrossing the foothills at the southern end of Rancho Corral de Tierra are no exception. Clipper Ridge and French trails are very steep, switchback-less tracks. Reward for the climb is a grand view of Montara Mountain to the north and Half Moon Bay to the south.

DIRECTIONS: From Highway 1, about 0.5 mile north of the traffic light in El Granada, turn inland on Coral Reef Avenue and follow it 0.3 steeply uphill to parking (and a tsunami evacuation site!).

THE HIKE: At a sign marking the boundary of Rancho CDT, ascend steeply on the dirt track. Give thanks to the volunteers who cut down the nonnative pampas grass that can make this trail impassable. The trail climbs to a football field-sized flat, where you can rest on a bench and contemplate the coastal view.

If you want more cardio workout and additional coastal views, continue another mile on Clipper Ridge Trail toward Scarpa Peak to an intersection with Deer Creek Trail. Otherwise, descend very steeply west on unsigned French Trail. After the trail turns south, it undergoes a personality change and becomes a pleasant path over wooden footbridges back to the trailhead.

Explore more of Rancho Corral de Tierra, a park-in-progress, known mostly to locals.

Vikram Seth's 'The Golden Gate' (1986), a novel in verse (sonnets written in iambic tetrameter to be precise), follows a group of yuppies in 1980s' San Francisco. The intricate stanzas are smart, fluid, witty (well-done puns and wordplay) and capture the flavor of the time.

EVERY TRAIL TELLS A STORY.

Golden Gate National Parklands Stories

HIKE ON.

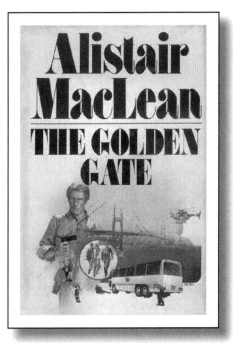

In *Alistair MacLean's* best-selling novel,
'The Golden Gate' (1976), a team of
criminals kidnaps the President of the
United States on the Golden Gate Bridge
and wire the bridge with explosives.
Unless they get half a billion dollars
ransom, they'll detonate the explosives,
which will kill the President and destroy
the Golden Gate Bridge.

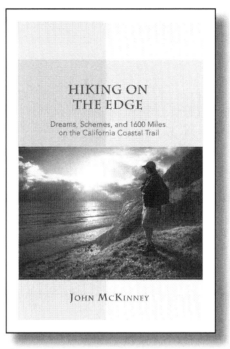

Marin Trails

From the chapter "Marin Trails" in *Hiking on the Edge: Dreams, Schemes and 1600 Miles on the California Coastal Trail* by John McKinney

From a hillside above Rodeo Lagoon, I peer down at the egrets, herons, and pelicans at water's edge, as well as the harbor seals and sea lions swimming in the surf and resting on the rocks. Up and over Wolf Ridge I travel to Tennessee Cove where, on a dark and stormy night, the side-wheel steamship Tennessee, with 600 passengers aboard, ran aground off this isolated cove. No radar, not even a lighthouse in those days. Fortunately, no lives were lost on that foggy night in 1853.

North of Tennessee Cove is as soul-satisfying a length of Coastal Trail as I've hiked on my entire journey. Oh, if only I could multiply by four hundred the three miles of trail from Tennessee Cove to Muir Beach and make all of the California Coastal Trail resemble this lupine-lined pathway etched onto the edge of bold cliffs.

I cross a footbridge over the mouth of a creek to Muir Beach, a wide expanse of coarse sand punctuated by big boulders. A half mile of trail leads inland to Muir Beach, the town, consisting of about one hundred homes scattered in the woodsy bluffs and exactly one business—the Pelican Inn, a very authentic English pub. Here I enjoy a shepherd's pie and a pint of ale, while imagining how much my English spirit guide, Joseph Smeaton Chase, would appreciate the sixteenth century look and feel of the inn.

An hour's tramp along a creekside (and, alas, roadside) path brings me to Muir Woods National Monument. I arrive just as dozens, in fact, hundreds of visitors rush for the park exit and parking lot and pile onto waiting tour buses. With the hope that those who made the trip had a more leisurely exploration of, than exodus from, the woods, I walk the wide main trail into the redwood cathedral. I was prepared to walk amongst the wonderful redwood groves with a multitude of admirers from around the world but appear to have unintentionally timed my visit to miss most of the crowd.

"You have done me a great honor and I am proud of it," wrote John Muir upon learning a redwood preserve was dedicated in his name. "This is the best tree-lover's monument that could possibly be found in all the forests of the world."

I quite agree with the great naturalist and enjoy my late afternoon walk along Redwood Creek. Surely my journey up-creek is far easier than that of the steelhead and salmon struggling upstream to spawn.

While John Muir provided the inspiration for setting aside these trees, it was California congressman and well-to-do conservationist Rep. William Kent who purchased 300 acres of virgin redwoods just in time to save them from the loggers' axes. He then persuaded President Theodore Roosevelt to declare the grove a national monument and name it for Muir. There's something to be said for this kind of early-twentieth century environmental action: one politically connected man of means, acting unilaterally, simply buys a threatened natural treasure and donates it to the public.

Jack Kerouac Hikes to Marin

In the Spring of 1956, poet Gary Snyder invited his buddy Jack Kerouac to stay with in his mountain shack and together they wandered the trails of Marin. Snyder (dubbed "Japhy") and their hikes became memorialized in Kerouac's 1956 classic *The Dharma Bums*. A few short quotes from his work follow.

...Japhy and I sneaked our rucksacks out, with a few choice groceries, and started down the road in the orange early-morning sun of California golden days. It was going to be a great day, we were back in our element: trails.

The Marin country was much more rustic and kindly than the rough Sierra country we'd climbed last fall: it was all flowers, trees, bushes, but also a great deal of poison oak by the side of the trail. When we got to the end of the high dirt road we suddenly plunged into the dense redwood forest and went along following a pipeline through glades that were so deep the fresh morning sun barely penetrated and it was cold and damp.

We...dipped down again through bushes to a trail that probably nobody even knew was there except a few hikers, and we were in Muir Woods. It extended, a vast valley, for miles before us. An old logger Road led us for two miles then Japhy got off and scrambled up the slope and got onto another trail nobody dreamed was there. We hiked on this one up and down along a tumbling creek, with fallen logs again where you cross the creek, and sometimes bridges that had been built Jaffe said by the Boy Scouts, trees sawed in half the flat surface for walking.

On this trip Jaffe had brought along a delicious combination for hiking energy: Ry-crisp crackers, good sharp cheddar cheese a wedge of that and a roll of salami. We had this for breakfast with hot fresh tea and felt great. Two grown men could live two days on that concentrated bread and that salami (concentrated meat) and cheese the whole thing only weighed about a pound and a half.

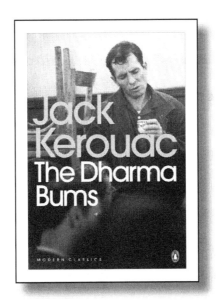

Marin-An by Gary Snyder

Gary Snyder (born May 8, 1930), best known as a poet of the Beat Generation and sometimes as the "Poet Laureate of Deep Ecology." The work of the Pulitzer Prize winning poet, as well as his essays and environmental activism, reflects his profound connection to nature and Buddhist spirituality. Below is an excerpt from his poem, "Marin-An."

distant dogs bark, a pair of

cawing crows; the twang

of a pygmy nuthatch high in a pine—

from behind the cypress windrow

the mare moves up, grazing.

a soft continuous roar

comes out of the far valley

of the six-lane highway—thousands

and thousands of cars

driving men to work.

Every Picture Tells a Story
Explore the history of the Golden Gate National Parklands through a diverse collection of historic and contemporary images on display in a gallery on the Golden Gate National Recreation Area web site. Photo collections include Alcatraz, Fort Point, Golden Gate Bridge, Marin Parklands, Muir Woods, the Presidio and more. The region's military history is particularly well documented in photographs.

The Presidio looked like a pretty nice place to be posted in 1915.

Ranger Card shares compass how-to with kids on the Marin Headlands, circa 1980.

Alcatraz Movies

Infamous Alcatraz has remained a part of our popular culture for many years after its closure and spawned at least four major motion pictures. These "Alcatraz films" are quite entertaining, though, if you're looking for historical accuracy, you should read a book.

"Escape from Alcatraz" (1979), starring Clint Eastwood, dramatizes a 1962 escape attempt from the prison, supposedly "escape proof" due to the cold water, strong currents, and circling sharks around the island. Did the Anglin brothers and Frank Lee Morris succeed? No trace of them was ever found.

"The Rock" (1996), a box office hit starring Sean Connery, Ed Harris, and Nicholas Cage, was filmed on the island. The action thriller tells the story of a team of SEALS assigned to break into Alcatraz, where rogue military men have taken tourists hostage and are threatening to launch rockets filled with nerve gas on San Francisco unless their ransom demands are met.

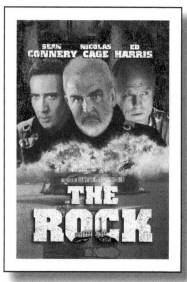

"Birdman of Alcatraz" (1962) tells the story of the two-time killer and so-called "Birdman" Robert Stroud, who found an injured bird in the prison yard and went on to become a world expert in ornithology. The intense prison drama, directed by John Frankenheimer, stars Burt Lancaster (Oscar nominated for Best Actor) and features Karl Malden as the warden and Telly Savalas as a fellow con.

"Murder in the First" (1995), a legal drama starring Kevin Bacon, Christian Slater and Gary Oldman, was inspired by the true story of petty criminal Henri Young sent to Alcatraz and later tried for murder in the first degree. His lawyer's defense attempted to put the prison itself on trial, arguing that the horrible conditions at Alcatraz drove prisoners insane.

Noted Literary Quotes about the Golden Gate Bridge

From Thomas Pynchon's *Vineland*:
Crossing the Golden Gate Bridge represents a transition, in the metaphysics of the region, there to be felt even by travelers unwary as Zoyd. When the busful of northbound hippies first caught sight of it, just at sundown as the fog was pouring in, the towers and cables ascending into pale gold otherworldly billows, you heard a lot of "Wow," and "Beautiful," though Zoyd only found it beautiful the way a firearm is, because of the bad dream unreleased inside it, in this case the brute simplicity of height, the finality of what swept below relentlessly out to sea. They rose into the strange gold smothering, visibility down to half a car length. . . .

From Dave Eggers' *A Heartbreaking Work of Staggering Genius*:
"Up there we see everything, Oakland to the left, El Cerrito and Richmond to the right, Marin forward, over the Bay, Berkeley below, all red rooftops and trees of cauliflower and columbine, shaped like rockets and explosions, all those people below us, with humbler views; we see the Bay Bridge, clunkety, the Richmond Bridge, straight, low, the Golden Gate, red toothpicks and string, the blue between, the blue above, the gleaming white Land of the Lost/Superman's North Pole Getaway magic crystals that are San Francisco."

From Jack London's Martin *Eden*:
Far Tamalpais, barely seen in the silver haze, bulked
hugely by the Golden Gate, the latter a pale gold
pathway under the westering sun. Beyond, the Pacific,
dime and vast, was raising on its sky-line tumbled
cloud-masses that swept landward, giving warming of
the first blustering breath of winter.

From Vikram Seth's *The Golden Gate*:

the towers,

High built, red-gold, with their long span

—The most majestic spun by man—

Whose threads of steel through mists and showers,

Wind, spray, and the momentous roar

Of ocean storms, link shore to shore.

From Fae Myenne Ng's *Bone*:
Late afternoon, Mason came and took us all for a
ride. He drove over the Golden Gate Bridge because he knew Mah loved how the light bounced off
the cable, copper and bright gold, and Leon like to
remember the first time he sailed into San Francisco,
how when his ship passed under the Golden Gate, th
light disappeared for a long moment.

Chief Engineer Joseph B. Strauss led the talented team that designed the iconic Golden Gate Bridge. He was the visionary, promoter and construction supervisor of the bridge, and, in his spare time, a poet. He penned "The Mighty Task is Done" upon completion of the building of the Bridge in May 1937.

At last the mighty task is done;
Resplendent in the western sun
The Bridge looms mountain high;
Its titan piers grip ocean floor,
Its great steel arms link shore with shore,
Its towers pierce the sky.

On its broad decks in rightful pride,
The world in swift parade shall ride,
Throughout all time to be;
Beneath, fleet ships from every port,
Vast landlocked bay, historic fort,
And dwarfing all—the sea.

To north, the Redwood Empire's gates;
'To south, a happy playground waits,
in Rapturous appeal;
Here nature, free since time began,
Yields to the restless moods of man,
Accepts his bonds of steel.

Launched midst a thousand hopes and fears,
Damned by a thousand hostile sneers,
Yet ne'er its course was stayed,
But ask of those who met the foe
Who stood alone when faith was low,
Ask them the price they paid.

Ask of the steel, each strut and wire,
Ask of the searching, purging fire,
That marked their natal hour;
Ask of the mind, the hand, the heart,
Ask of each single, stalwart part,
What gave it force and power.

An Honored cause and nobly fought
And that which they so bravely wrought,
Now glorifies their deed,
No selfish urge shall stain its life,
Nor envy, greed, intrigue, nor strife,
Nor false, ignoble creed.

High overhead its lights shall gleam,
Far, far below life's restless stream,
Unceasingly shall flow;
For this was spun its lithe fine form,
To fear not war, nor time, nor storm,
For Fate had meant it so.

Death Valley NP
LAVA BEDS NM
YOSEMITE NATIONAL PARK
Pinnacles NP
Joshua Tree National Park
EUGENE O'NEILL NHS
MUIR WOODS NM
Whiskeytown-Shasta Trinity NRA
Golden Gate National Recreation Area
REDWOOD NP
CHANNEL ISLANDS NATIONAL PARK
DEVILS POSTPILE NM
LASSEN VOLCANIC NATIONAL PARK
Cabrillo NM
MOJAVE NPRES
César Chávez NM
John Muir NHS
Rosie the Riveter NHS
Santa Monica Mountains NRA
POINT REYES NS
SEQUOIA-KINGS CANYON NATIONAL PARKS

CALIFORNIA'S
NATIONAL PARKS

Other states have national parks with tall trees, high peaks, deep canyons, long seashores and vast deserts, but only California can claim all these grand landscapes within its boundaries.

California boasts nine national parks, the most in the nation. In addition, the state's national parklands include national recreation areas, national monuments, national historic parks, a national seashore and a national preserve.

The state features one of America's oldest national parks—Yosemite set aside in 1890—and one of its newest—César E. Chávez National Monument established in 2012.

Mere acreage does not a national park make, but California's national parks include the largest park in the contiguous U.S.—3.3-million acre Death Valley National Park. Yosemite (748,542 acres) and Joshua Tree (790,636 acres) are also huge by any park standards. Even such smaller parklands as Redwoods National Park and Pt. Reyes National Seashore are by no means small.

California and The National Park Idea

Not long after John Muir walked through Mariposa Grove and into the Yosemite Valley, California's natural treasures attracted attention worldwide and conservationists rallied to preserve them as parks. As the great naturalist put it in 1898: "Thousands of nerve-shaken, overcivilized people are beginning to find out that going to the mountains is going home; that wilderness is a necessity; and that mountain parks and reservations are useful not only as fountains of timber and irrigating rivers, but as fountains of life."

The National Park Service, founded in 1916, was initially guided by borax tycoon-turned-park-champion Stephen T. Mather and his young assistant, California attorney Horace Albright. The park service's mission was the preservation of "the scenery and the natural and historic objects and the wild life" and the provision "for the enjoyment of the same in such manner and by such means as will leave them unimpaired for the enjoyment of future generations."

The invention of the automobile revolutionized national park visitation, particularly in car-conscious California. John Muir called them "blunt-nosed mechanical beetles," yet as one California senator pointed out, "If Jesus Christ had an automobile he wouldn't have ridden a jackass into Jerusalem."

With cars came trailers, and with trailer camps came concessionaires. National parks filled with mobile cities of canvas and aluminum, and by visitors anxious to see California's natural wonders. During the 1920s and 30s, the park service constructed signs identifying scenic features and rangers assumed the role of interpreting nature for visitors.

By 1930 California had four national parks: Yosemite, Lassen, Sequoia and General Grant (Kings Canyon.) In the 1930s, two big desert areas—Joshua Tree and Death Valley—became national monuments.

With the 1960s came hotly contested, and eventually successful campaigns to create Redwood National

Steven Mather (R) and his assistant Horace Albright guided the National Park Service in its early days.

Park and Point Reyes National Seashore. During the 1970s the National Park Service established parks near the state's big cities—Golden Gate National Recreation Area on the San Francisco waterfront and Marin headlands and Santa Monica Mountains National Recreation Area, a Mediterranean ecosystem near Los Angeles. Also during that decade, Mineral King Valley was saved from a mega-ski resort development and added to Sequoia National Park. Channel Islands National Park, an archipelago offshore from Santa Barbara, was established in 1980.

During the 1980s and 1990s, major conservation battles raged in the desert. After more than two decades of wrangling, Joshua Tree and Death Valley national monuments were greatly expanded and given national park status, and the 1.6-million acre Mojave National Preserve was established under provisions of the 1994 California Desert Conservation Act.

Today, the National Park Service must address challenging questions: How best to regulate concessionaires? Should motor vehicles be banned from Yosemite Valley? How can aging park facilities cope with many years of deferred maintenance?

And the biggest issue of all: How will our parks (indeed our planet!) cope with the rapidly increasing effects of climate change?

The consequences of climate change to California's national parks is ever more apparent. In recent years, after prolonged droughts, devastating wildfires burned the Yosemite backcountry, parts of Sequoia National Park and more than half the Santa Monica Mountains National Recreation Area. Scientists have discovered that trees in Sequoia and Kings Canyon national parks endure the worst ozone levels of all national parks, in part because of their proximity to farm-belt air in the San Joaquin Valley.

California's national parklands struggle with an ever-increasing numbers of visitors. The California Office of Tourism charts visitation to national parks along with airports, hotel occupancy and other attractions such as Disneyland and Universal Studios. Yosemite is California's most-visited park with 4.5 to 5 million visitors a year, and many other parks count millions of visitors or "visitor days," per year.

What may be the saving grace of national parks is the deep-seated, multi-generational pride Americans have for their national parklands. We not only love national parks, we love the very idea of national parks. Even in an era of public mistrust toward government, national parks remain one of the most beloved institutions of American life.

National Parks have often been celebrated as America's best idea. As writer Wallace Stegner put it: "National parks are the best idea we ever had. Absolutely American, absolutely democratic, they reflect us at our best rather than our worst."

The Trails

The state of the state's national park trail system is excellent. Trailhead parking, interpretive panels and displays, as well as signage, is generally tops in the field. Backcountry junctions are usually signed and trail conditions, with a few exceptions of course, range from good to excellent.

Trail systems evolved on a park-by-park basis and it's difficult to speak in generalities about their respective origins. A good deal of Yosemite's trail system was in place before the early horseless carriages chugged into the park.

Several national parks were aided greatly by the Depression-era Civilian Conservation Corps of the 1930s. Sequoia and Pinnacles national parks, for example, have hand-built trails by the CCC that are true gems, highlighted by stonework and bridges that would no doubt be prohibitively expensive to construct today.

Scout troops, the hard-working young men and women of the California Conservation Corps and many volunteer groups are among the organizations that help park staff build and maintain trails.

The trail system in California's national parklands shares many characteristics in common with pathways overseen by other governmental bodies, and have unique qualities as well. One major difference between national parks and, for example, California's state parks, is the amount of land preserved as wilderness. A majority of Yosemite, Sequoia, Death Valley, Joshua Tree and several more parks are official federally designated wilderness. Wilderness comprises some 94 percent of Yosemite National Park, 93 percent of Death Valley National Park, and more than 80 percent of Joshua Tree National Park.

On national park maps you'll find wilderness areas delineated as simply "Wilderness." Unlike the Forest Service, the Bureau of Land Management or other wilderness stewards, the National Park Service does not name its wilderness areas.

Author John McKinney admires the sign for Yosemite's Four Mile Trail.

"Wilderness" is more than a name for a wild area. By law, a wilderness is restricted to non-motorized entry—that is to say, equestrian and foot travel. Happily, hikers do not have to share the trails with snowmobiles or mountain bikes in national park wilderness.

Because national park trails attract visitors from all over the globe, the park service makes use of international symbols on its signage, and the metric system as well. Don't be surprised if you spot trail signs with distance expressed in kilometers as well as miles and elevation noted in meters as well as feet.

The hikers you meet on a national park trail may be different from the company you keep on trails near home. California's national parks attract increasing numbers of ethnically and culturally diverse hikers of all ages, shapes and sizes, from across the nation and around the world. Once I counted ten languages on a popular trail in Yosemite! The hiking experience is much enriched by sharing the trail with hikers from literally all walks of life.

California's National Parklands

Alcatraz Island
Cabrillo National Monument
Castle Mountains National Monument
César E. Chávez National Monument
Channel Islands National Park
Death Valley National Park
Devils Postpile National Monument
Eugene O'Neill National Historic Site
Fort Point National Historic Site
Golden Gate National Recreation Area
John Muir National Historic Site
Joshua Tree National Park
Lassen Volcanic National Park
Lava Beds National Monument
Manzanar National Historic Site
Mojave National Preserve
Muir Woods National Monument
Pinnacles National Park
Point Reyes National Seashore
Port Chicago Naval Magazine National Memorial
Presidio of San Francisco
Redwood National and State Parks
Rosie the Riveter WWII Home Front National
    Historic Park
San Francisco Maritime National Historic Park
Santa Monica Mountains National Recreation Area
Sequoia and Kings Canyon National Parks
Tule Lake National Monument
Whiskeytown National Recreation Area
Yosemite National Park

The Hiker's Index

Celebrating the Scenic, Sublime and Sensational Points of Interest in California's National Parks

State with the most National Parks

California, with 9

Largest National Park in Contiguous U.S.

Death Valley with 3.3 million acres

Third Largest National Park in Contiguous U.S.

Mojave National Preserve

Foggiest Place on the West Coast

Point Reyes Lighthouse, Point Reyes National Seashore

World's Tallest Tree

A 379.7-foot high coast redwood named Hyperion in Redwood National Park

World's Largest Tree

General Sherman Tree, 275 feet tall, with a base circumference of 102 feet, growing in the Giant Forest Area of Sequoia National Park

World's Largest-In-Diameter Tree

General Grant Tree, dubbed "the nation's Christmas tree," more than 40 feet in diameter at its base, growing in Kings Canyon National Park.

Largest Elephant Seal Population on Earth

San Miguel Island, Channel Islands National Park

Highest Point in Contiguous U.S.

Mt. Whitney (14,508 feet in elevation) on the far eastern boundary of Sequoia National Park

Lowest Point in Western Hemisphere

Badwater (282 feet below sea level) in Death Valley National Park

California's Largest Island

Santa Cruz Island, Channel Islands National Park

Only Major Metropolis Bisected by a Mountain Range

Los Angeles, by the Santa Monica Mountains (National Recreation Area)

Highest Waterfall in North America

Yosemite Falls, at 2,425 feet, in Yosemite National Park

JOHN MCKINNEY

John McKinney is an award-winning writer, public speaker, and author of 30 hiking-themed books: inspiring narratives, top-selling guides, books for children.

John is particularly passionate about sharing the stories of California trails. He is the only one to have visited—and written about—all 280 California State Parks. John tells the story of his epic hike along the entire California coast in the critically acclaimed *Hiking on the Edge: Dreams, Schemes, and 1600 Miles on the California Coastal Trail.*

For 18 years John, aka The Trailmaster, wrote a weekly hiking column for the Los Angeles Times, and has hiked and enthusiastically told the story of more than 10 thousand miles of trail across California and around the world. His "Every Trail Tells a Story" series of guides highlight the very best hikes in California.

The intrepid Eagle Scout has written more than a thousand stories and opinion pieces about hiking, parklands, and our relationship with nature.

A passionate advocate for hiking and our need to reconnect with nature, John is a frequent public speaker, and shares his tales on radio, on video, and online.

JOHN MCKINNEY:
"EVERY TRAIL TELLS A STORY."

HIKE ON.

TheTrailmaster.com

Made in the USA
Columbia, SC
22 April 2022